W9-CMB-587

AMERICAN FLANNEL

ALSO BY STEVEN KURUTZ

Like a Rolling Stone: The Strange Life of a Tribute Band

AMERICAN FLANNEL

How a Band of Entrepreneurs
Are Bringing the Art and Business
of Making Clothes Back Home

Steven Kurutz

RIVERHEAD BOOKS | *New York* | 2024

RIVERHEAD BOOKS
An imprint of Penguin Random House LLC
penguinrandomhouse.com

Copyright © 2024 by Steven Kurutz
Penguin Random House supports copyright. Copyright fuels creativity,
encourages diverse voices, promotes free speech, and creates a vibrant culture.
Thank you for buying an authorized edition of this book and for complying with
copyright laws by not reproducing, scanning, or distributing any part of it in any
form without permission. You are supporting writers and allowing Penguin
Random House to continue to publish books for every reader.

Riverhead and the R colophon are registered trademarks of
Penguin Random House LLC.

Some portions of this book were previously published in
substantially different forms in *The New York Times* as
"The Annals of Flannel" and "The Sock Queen of Alabama."

Library of Congress Cataloging-in-Publication Data
Names: Kurutz, Steven, author.
Title: American flannel: how a band of entrepreneurs are bringing the art
and business of making clothes back home / Steven Kurutz.
Description: New York: Riverhead Books, 2024. |
Identifiers: LCCN 2023039150 (print) | LCCN 2023039151 (ebook) |
ISBN 9780593329610 (hardcover) | ISBN 9780593329634 (ebook)
Subjects: LCSH: American Giant (Firm) | Clothing trade—
United States—History—21st century. | Textile industry—
United States—History—21st century. | Flannel—United States—
History—21st century. | Manufacturing industries—
United States—History—21st century.
Classification: LCC HD9940.U6 A445 2024 (print) | LCC HD9940.U6 (ebook) |
DDC 338.4/76870973—dc23/eng/20230830
LC record available at https://lccn.loc.gov/2023039150
LC ebook record available at https://lccn.loc.gov/2023039151

Printed in the United States of America
1st Printing

Book design by Cassandra Garruzzo Mueller

For Cara
and for her father, Stephen Dorr

CONTENTS

AMERICAN FLANNEL

The 2 Percent

I n 1989, the American workwear brand Carhartt produced a special clothing collection to mark its centennial in business. While shopping with my wife at a vintage store in Lambertville, New Jersey, a few years ago, I came across one of these garments—a cotton-duck work jacket with a patch on the chest pocket that read "100 Years, 1889–1989." The same was embossed on each brass button. Intrigued, I took the jacket off its hanger and studied it more closely. The inside was lined with a blanketlike fabric to provide extra warmth when working outdoors. "Crafted with Pride in U.S.A." read the neck label, and the underside bore the insignia of the United Garment Workers of America, a labor union founded around the same time as Carhartt itself. Nineteen eighty-nine doesn't seem that long ago. But holding this jacket in my hands, I began to have the feeling you get when looking at a very old photograph. I was holding an artifact from a lost world.

It wasn't simply the reference to the trade union, which ceased to exist not long after the jacket was made. Or that modern work coats rarely have the practical feature of a blanket lining because it adds to production costs. It was that the country's entire apparel-making industry had all but vanished in the decades since. We still wore blue jeans, high-top sneakers, Western boots, button-down dress shirts, and durable workwear, all of which are American inventions, but we no longer produced them. Most clothing, Carhartt's included, was now made in low-cost factories around the world, principally in Asia. The statistics tell the harsh story. In 1980, around 70 percent of the clothing Americans wore was made domestically. Today, that figure is 2 percent. Over a period of forty years, America had out-sourced the shirt off its back.

⁕ ⁕⁕⁕⁕ ⁕

As a longtime Styles reporter for *The New York Times*, I covered the apparel industry, but only glancingly. I rarely attended fashion shows and never once spent a day trailing around after Ralph Lauren or Tom Ford for a profile. My interest was in how style was created and took shape in little-known, often unglamorous corners of the business. I wrote, for instance, about a retail liquidator in the South that sold heavily-marked-down Balenciaga and Chanel out of strip malls. Another story centered on a century-old family business, M&S Schmalberg, that made fabric flowers for Broadway costumers and fashion designers like Vera Wang and Marc Jacobs. The week I spent at the upper-floor factory in New York's Garment District, watching workers assemble the delicate creations with silk, wire, and craft glue, was more thrilling to me than sitting front row at Paris Fashion Week. Not long after I happened upon that Carhartt jacket, I began to think about garment manufacturing and why the United States, which once had a thriving apparel industry, no longer practiced these things. Clothing is a basic human need. What did it mean for a nation to lose the ability to make it on any scale?

Researching the subject, I came across the work of Christopher Payne, an architectural photographer who some years ago had made a project of documenting America's textile mills. Payne grew up in New England, where the country's textile, apparel, and shoe industries began in the late 1700s and flourished for a century and a half. The massive brick mills loom over the landscape, he told me. "The shadow of it—the weight—is strong." One day, Payne recalled, he was on the phone with a factory owner in the Massachusetts city of Fall River, which in the late nineteenth and early twentieth centuries had been a world leader in the production of cotton cloth. The man ran a cut-and-sew factory for men's shirts, making them for a variety of high-end brands. "There's one area of the building I can show you," he told Payne. "In that room, you're going to get one shot, and in that one shot, you will see the entire arc of the textile industry." Payne drove there eagerly. The factory was typical of the other mill buildings in the area: granite exterior, open floors, wood columns and beams, wood floors, wood stairwells. The factory occupied two floors of the building. The owner welcomed him inside and led him to the workspace. Payne expected to see a room filled with humming machinery and busy workers. Instead, he said, "You open this door and there was this giant hall, this vast space. And it was *empty*."

Payne was stunned speechless. "And the millowner looked at me and said, 'Gone to China.'"

At first, I dwelled on the 98 percent of clothing now made overseas, one more sorry outcome of America's decision, starting in the 1970s, to renounce its role as factory to the world and outsource to developing countries. But after a time, my focus reversed, and I became intrigued by not what was lost but what remained—the 2 percent, and those who were working to grow that number once again.

Apparel was one of the easiest industries to offshore. A sewing plant in Pennsylvania or North Carolina could be packed up whole, the machinery loaded onto a boat and shipped to Bangladesh or Indonesia, where eager workers would do the job for perhaps five dollars a day. Anyone who had fought against such economic forces was either stubborn or crazy or really good at what they did. All of those possibilities interested me, and I wondered, *Who still makes clothes in America? Who is bold enough to enter the industry now, and why? And how are they faring?*

My interest was with manufacturers, rather than tailors, knitters, or other artisans, because of the challenges of running a factory, and because the basic, well-built clothing that defined American style—blue jeans, for example—was made on an industrial scale. Through the mid-twentieth century, textiles and apparel had been one of the largest U.S. industries: in 1973, roughly the peak, more than 2.4 million Americans were employed in producing fabric and clothing of all kinds. But between the years 1990 and 2012, the apparel sector lost more than a million jobs, or more than three-quarters of its workforce, according to the Bureau of Labor Statistics. To be part of a business of that scale that virtually disappears in your lifetime—maybe even while you are trying to make a living at it—is a strange and rare experience. (As a newspaper reporter, I know a little of the feeling.) The 2 percent were, by definition, survivors. And those who had joined their ranks? I was curious to hear their stories.

Danny Swafford was one of them. He ran a cut-and-sew factory—an apparel workshop—in the town of Milledgeville, Tennessee, population 265. He started the business in 1979, at the dawn of the great wave offshore, and it specialized in men's and boy's sportswear and athletic apparel. Among many other things, Danny's factory had made soccer shorts for JCPenney, boxer shorts for Kmart, football uniforms for Riddell, athletic gear for Umbro, and a hooded zip-up jacket for Carhartt not unlike the one I found in the vintage store. All those clients had called him up at some point and told him, in so many words, "Sorry, we're pulling out." Reached by phone at his factory one afternoon, Danny elaborated: "They didn't say, 'We will leave you tomorrow.' They was all very nice. It's like landing an airplane—they just slowly go down. Then they'd call up and say, 'Well, in a couple of months, we can no longer, you know, manufacture here.'" Danny's factory went from 160 employees at its peak in the early '90s to himself and 10 others at present.

I found Danny through a small label that sold premium denim—his factory was known to produce clothes of superior quality—and if I expected him to be bitter or dejected by the state of things, he was not. He was upbeat and enthusiastic. At age seventy-two, he loved manufacturing clothes as much as he had when he was in high school and took a summer job making ladies' slacks at a company called Marlene Industries. The only things Danny loved as much as running an apparel factory were Tennessee football and Martha Stewart cooking shows. His factory had lately sewn blue jeans, children's clothes, and a line of stylish workwear for women, Gamine, producing for independent labels who valued "Made in America." He hustled constantly to get new clients. "I just always have found the apparel business fascinating," he said. "As long as it's still fun, I'm going to keep trucking on." He laughed. "I guess I'm a little different."

Actually, I came to see that Danny was not at all different. To my surprise, I kept meeting more people like him. Through his pride in making quality products locally and his perseverance in keeping his factory going despite enormous challenges, he exemplified the traits of his colleagues. Some, like Danny, were veterans of the days when the industry was booming. But a good number were newcomers who had improbably decided to forgo law or software engineering or some other, more lucrative field to manufacture clothing. These upstarts brought fresh energy to a battered industry, and they embraced modern technology and new ways of doing things to compete in a global marketplace of cheaply produced fast fashion.

They included an outspoken entrepreneur determined to revive classic, mass-produced sportswear and challenge Levi's and other big apparel brands; a woman who returned to her Alabama hometown to save her family's hosiery mill and, just possibly, her city's reputation as the onetime sock capital of the world; a son who joined his father in keeping alive the craft of handsewn shoemaking in Maine; and the chief executive of a denim label who envisioned a new, more sustainable way to grow cotton and make jeans domestically.

They were driven by personal history, by the desire to make products of lasting quality, by a sense of loyalty to American workers and communities. There was a contagiousness to it—one thus-minded entrepreneur inspired and enabled another. And as these strong-willed, resilient, clever, unusual Americans fought to keep their businesses going, or to start new ones, they nurtured in me a hope. That America, having become a nation of consumers and marketers, could once more be a place where people made things.

Chapter 1

A Committed Dude

The quest began as simply as this: growing up in the late 1970s, Bayard Winthrop had a favorite shirt.

The shirt was a cotton flannel, heavyweight, with a plaid pattern of blue, white, and gray. Bayard wore it to hockey practice in Greenwich, Connecticut, where he grew up. He took it along when he attended boarding school in Massachusetts. All through his boyhood, until he outgrew it, he wore that plaid flannel shirt. An item of clothing becomes cherished because it conjures special meanings and emotions for the wearer. Flannel made Bayard feel cool. "It looked great," he recalled, "and I thought it said something about me—that I was physical and capable and outdoorsy."

Admittedly, his name didn't exactly telegraph "rugged flannel shirt." Bayard (pronounced *BY-erd*) Winthrop is a descendant of one of the oldest and most distinguished families in America. A university, a hospital, a Harvard residence hall, and towns in Massachusetts and Maine were all named after his forebears. Bayard's great-great-great-great-great-great-great-great-great-grandfather, John Winthrop, was an English Puritan who became the first governor of the

Massachusetts Bay Colony. In 1630, before reaching the new world, he delivered the famous "City upon a Hill" sermon later quoted by several U.S. presidents, most famously Ronald Reagan in his 1980 election eve address to assert America's exceptionalism. A distant uncle, Robert Winthrop, was a noted philanthropist, sportsman, and conservationist who campaigned to save the mallard duck. Indeed, the family name carried the unmistakable ring of Yankee blue blood. Once, when he was in college, a professor calling roll quipped, "Bayard Winthrop—not a lot of history in *that* name."

Bayard's father, John, grew up on the north shore of Massachusetts and on Park Avenue, and like every man in his line going back generations, he attended Harvard. He went to work as a wealth manager for the family firm, Wood, Struthers & Winthrop. In the mid-1960s, he settled his young family into a big white Colonial on seven acres bordering "back country" Greenwich. Like his two older brothers, Jay and Grenville, Bayard was sent to the elite private school Greenwich Country Day. It was grooming for a comfortable life of profiting from an ever-upward climb in the stock market and enjoying cocktails and backslaps at the Round Hill Club. At some point along the success trajectory, the family name would be burnished through charitable giving and volunteer work.

But in 1976, when Bayard was seven, his parents divorced acrimoniously, and the picture of old-money comfort and privilege turned more complicated. John kept the estate and much of the couple's social circle, while Bayard's mother, Deborah, who had grown up adjacent to wealth but not of it, struggled to find her place as a newly single mother in a clubby town. Deborah and the children moved to a smaller house a few miles away that she received in the divorce settlement. She got her real estate license and eventually sold the house and pulled out the equity, moving her sons to a less affluent part of town. She would repeat that maneuver every few years throughout Bayard's childhood, selling and moving to another, often smaller house. Bayard began his life amid the rolling pastureland and fieldstone walls of the Connecticut countryside. Five moves and ten years later, home was a first-floor condo unit hard against the I-95 overpass.

Greenwich back then was more economically diverse than it is today. There was a Woolworth's on main street. Amid the old-money WASPs, there were middle-class neighborhoods where the tradespeople lived. Bayard and Gren lived with their mother (Jay had gone to live with their father) and they existed more in this workaday world. One of Deborah's longtime boyfriends drove a town car as a chauffeur. Another man in her social circle was a mechanic who rode a Harley Sportster. Gren opted to attend the public high school, where he was on the hockey team and hung out with a rowdy crowd. Deborah sometimes took in boarders to help pay the bills. The boys were semi-feral latchkey kids, mostly raising themselves while their mother worked and struggled to cope emotionally. They dubbed one of their favorite dinners—vinegar poured over saltine crackers—"super sogs."

Aside from that favorite flannel shirt, Bayard didn't show much interest in clothes. He was a heavy kid, so most clothing didn't flatter him, and he was never very materialistic. His mother told me that Bayard's eldest brother, Jay, was the sharp dresser in the family, sporting a khakis-and-polos East Coast Ivy look. "Whereas Bayard," she said, "I once looked in his closet, and I said, 'Bayard! You haven't got four pieces of clothing.'"

John continued to pay for Bayard's education, and at fourteen he was sent away to boarding school in Deerfield, Massachusetts. Back home on breaks, whatever house they were living in at the time became party central for Bayard, Gren, and their buddies. Bayard was boisterous and physical; moving back and forth between two very different worlds left him feeling that he didn't quite belong in the one where the Winthrops had always stood.

In his teens, Bayard spent a lot of time at the houses of his friends, in a sense adopted by more stable families. The Kendalls were one such family. Don Kendall, the father of Kent Kendall, Bayard's close friend from Country Day, was a self-made success who had grown up on a dairy farm and served as a navy pilot during World War II. Don went to work for PepsiCo as a delivery driver after being discharged and rose through the corporate ranks to become chief executive. He earned renown as the boardroom mastermind behind the cola wars of the 1980s. "Even though he was a CEO, my dad was very present," Kent Kendall told me. "He was playing football with us. Breaking out the snowmobile or taking us on the tractor. Bayard was probably like, 'Wow, this is what a happy family and an engaged dad looks like.' He was definitely looking for that." Mr. Kendall, as Bayard continued to call him even as an adult, became a role model, a blend of old-fashioned bootstrapping and exceptional achievement in business.

When it came time for college, Bayard made a halfhearted attempt to follow in the Winthrop tradition and applied to Harvard, but he'd been an underachieving and directionless student and was waitlisted. He ended up at the University of Vermont, where he came into himself. Bayard's college friends told me that between his sophomore and junior years, an engine of ambition kicked in. He spent a month in Wyoming's Wind River Range as part of a course at the National Outdoor Leadership School, lost a bunch of weight, and set his sights on Wall Street. After interning at Donaldson, Lufkin & Jenrette for two summers, Bayard was accepted into the New York investment bank's prestigious trainee program following graduation, in 1991. He shared a tiny Upper East Side walkup with a college buddy who also worked in finance and a childhood friend from Greenwich. Dressed in a suit and tie, he logged grueling eighty-hour workweeks as a junior analyst. He still didn't care about clothes, but occasionally a colleague's footwear would catch his eye in the elevator. "Every now and then," he said, "I'd find a great pair of shoes and go, 'Those are *awesome fucking shoes!*'"

Bayard soon grew to dislike Wall Street's culture of macho bluster and punishing workloads, however. "Friday afternoons," he recalled, "there was this staffing guy there. He would wander the halls and look for any analyst that didn't have smoke coming off their computer and assign them stuff. Like ruining your weekends." It instilled a work ethic that has served him well, "But the part I didn't like was it reminded me of the fraternities in college. This idea that you were rewarded for acting really busy as opposed to the actual work." He also found life in New York confining; he longed for a pickup truck and a dog. In 1993, after two unhappy years, he quit his finance career and left the city, turning away from the Winthrop path for good. His plan was to drive cross-country to Seattle and work construction, but then an old friend happened to call. As they chatted, the friend remarked on the new lightness in Bayard's voice. "You don't have any interest in moving to San Francisco, do you?" the friend asked. "I'm moving out there, and I want a roommate."

Here's what Bayard *was* interested in: working for a company that inspired him. He wanted a tangible output to his day, to produce *real* things—no more selling institutional investors on corporate debt. In San Francisco, he learned through his roommate about a tiny company, Atlas Snowshoe, whose signature product was a spring-loaded binding that reduced drag as you walked. He'd never gone snowshoeing in his life. But it was a product, and the hands-on nature of the enterprise—"a couple of guys in a fucking warehouse in a shitty part of San Francisco making it happen," as he put it— appealed to him. He spent months begging the founders for a job. "I was like, 'Hire me, hire me. I'll clean your fucking toilets.'"

Short and boxy through the trunk, with bristly cropped hair and a ruddy complexion, Bayard had the physical appearance and scrappy intensity of a wrestler. Atlas hired him, and he never stopped working. Now that he'd found his purpose, he was bursting with energy, ideas, and opinions. Always strong opinions. He eventually managed sales, customer service, and production for Atlas. He made peanuts compared with his old Wall Street salary, but, he said, "I fucking loved it. It felt so real to me in a way that investment banking had not."

In 1996, Bayard left Atlas and networked himself into a job as president of one of the first webchat sites. It was an internet start-up with no product, but he figured it was the next logical career step to becoming a hotshot Bay Area CEO. "It was the first internet wave, and there were all these search engines like Yahoo and Infoseek. Everybody believed that sticky audiences were everything—and we had a huge audience. They would stay online for like ninety minutes a session because they're talking about right-wing politics or whatever the hell they're talking about." He got two valuable things out of the experience: a million-dollar windfall when the company was sold to Disney a few years later and the realization that he was not destined to be the next Silicon Valley wunderkind. "I hated this internet chat community shit."

In 2001, Bayard returned to the product world, this time as co-head of a skateboard company, Freebord. (He wasn't a skater, either.) Invented by a Stanford-educated engineer named Steen Strand, the Freebord itself was a weird evolution of a skateboard, with six wheels that mimicked the sliding motion of a snowboard, but on pavement. The company assembled the boards at its warehouse headquarters, although in time, to cut costs, it hired a Chinese factory to make the skate trucks. Bayard again worked tirelessly to build Freebord into the next big thing, with only marginal success. "For people who had the fearlessness to do it, they fell in love with it," he said. "But the learning curve was massive. And it was dangerous and shit. Anyway, that consumed eight years of my life."

His next job, running the accessories brand Chrome Industries, proved to be his crucible. The moment when, as Bayard said, he "got conviction" around his American-made ethos. He was thirty-nine.

It was 2008, and the country's culture was going through a transformation. In the '80s and '90s, if a chain like Olive Garden or the Gap opened in your town, you'd made the big time. But now, many people, especially in coastal cities, were turning away from mass production and mass culture, instead seeking out the artisanal, the small-batch, the handcrafted. Farm-to-table restaurants were opening around the nation, along with craft breweries and coffee shops that served certified-organic beans roasted on-site. Bayard saw it all around him in San Francisco, an epicenter of the maker and locavore movements. When the global financial crisis struck, plunging the country into a deep recession, many people began to rethink their spending habits, including on clothing. The new chic was investing in a few select pieces of superior quality, rather than buying cheap stuff to be worn a couple of times and then tossed. For those who could afford it, fast fashion was out. Heirloom was in.

The dominant fashion trend during this period was the heritage movement. Enduring American labels like Woolrich, Carhartt, Filson, and Red Wing were being rediscovered and revived by cool tastemakers living in places like Brooklyn and Portland. Having grown up in rural Pennsylvania among hunters, I can well remember my surprise at seeing young men, many of them with bushy beards, walking around downtown Manhattan dressed in buffalo-plaid shirts and heavy leather work boots, looking like they were going off to a deer camp, not an office building. The "heritage" look—the term was a nod to both vintage styles and long-lived,

heritage-worthy brands—came into vogue around 2006 and dominated men's fashion for nearly a decade. Some women adopted the
look, too, wearing Carhartt coats and beanies. It was popular not
only on the coasts but also in the middle of the country, where regular guys found that they didn't have to reorient their entire identity
or risk looking silly to be on trend. After all, they were wearing
their grandfathers' clothes. Buying a classic chore coat you would
own for the next fifty years was good value, too.

A photographer from Texas went around the country documenting local factories and artisans for what he dubbed the American
Craftsman Project. A former theology student taught himself to sew,
started making jeans in a Cincinnati workshop, and founded the
label Noble Denim. A group of surfers who loved Birdwell Beach
Britches, the old-school Southern California surfwear brand, bought
the sleepy company and its factory and reinvented it for a new generation. In those years, every week brought more stories like these.
The original heritage brands also caught on to the trend, opening
their archives and partnering with up-and-coming designers to re-
lease capsule collections that reworked their classics. For instance,
Woolrich hired Daiki Suzuki, the Japanese founder of the label
Engineered Garments, to produce a spin-off collection, Woolrich
Woolen Mills. And the designer Todd Snyder created a boutique for
J. Crew called the Liquor Store, housed in a former bar in Lower
Manhattan, which became a retail temple to all things heritage wear.
Aside from quality, a big part of the appeal was that the clothes had
long been, or were still, made in America.

The heritage movement could seem a little affected at times. As
a writer for *Newsweek* noted wryly, young men were buying clothes

"originally meant for mining or fishing, then wearing them to tapas bars and contemporary art installations." Some adopters of the style went around dressing and behaving as if the twentieth century had never happened. At one point, a barbershop in Williamsburg did a brisk business giving shaves with a straight razor, and a boutique in Tribeca sold handmade hatchets sourced from a secret workshop in Maine—peak trend. Still, the underlying impulse was genuine: a desire for timeless quality in a disposable culture, a search for value during lean times, an appreciation of classic American goods.

The new ethos of quality appealed to Bayard, who had always exhibited an affinity for extreme thrift and an aversion to waste, like some latter-day child of the Depression. Even after he became an executive, he bought his outdated clothes at Goodwill. He drove an old Toyota pickup truck that was dented and patched. Sticky notes slapped on the dash were his version of a daily planner. Rather than splurge on luxury vacations or dine at trendy restaurants, he liked to hang out with his dog, Bart, a yellow Lab who rode in the back of the truck wherever he went. Alice Roche, a jewelry designer who later became Bayard's wife, recalled their first date. Bayard took her to Gaspare's Pizza House, an old-school spot with red-gingham tablecloths near Golden Gate Park. At the end of the meal, there were a few slices left over. "He started putting everything in the box," Alice said. "He put in the bread rolls. Then he took the little butter pats. I remember looking at him, thinking, *Why is he taking all this stuff?*" She laughed. "He would have taken the water if he could have put it in the box!"

Chrome, the company over which Bayard now presided, had been founded in Boulder, Colorado, in the mid-1990s by two avid cyclists who started making messenger bags. Its signature product was the Citizen, a bag with a sturdy metal buckle that snapped across the chest seatbelt-style. It was popular with urban bike messengers because it was pretty much indestructible, made from military-grade tarpaulin. Chrome's factories, in Colorado and Chico, California, operated much like artisan workshops: bags came out with slight flaws, which gave them a handmade quality prized by customers. Each had its own charmingly imperfect character, and the brand produced special editions for its loyal fans. Anne Dupuis quit her job at a Chicago bike shop and moved to San Francisco, where Chrome had relocated in the early 2000s, to work for the label. "We did a custom art series with local artists," she said. "We'd be like, 'We want lime green with hot-pink vinyl.' We could do cool shit."

In 2007, Chrome was bought by Rory Fuerst Sr., a serial entrepreneur who had made a small fortune refurbishing worn-out sneakers for joggers during the 1970s running boom, then a bigger fortune in the early 2000s as a founder of the footwear brand Keen. After Bayard was brought in, he was tasked with turning the tiny bag company into a label that would appeal to a much larger base of customers. The plan was to expand into apparel, add shoes, get the products carried by REI and other chain retailers, and build Chrome into a multimillion-dollar business like Keen.

An idea began to form in Bayard's mind, a way to turn American-made craftsmanship into the focus of the company's philosophy. Chrome would be a modern version of a heritage brand, selling authentic goods of superior quality. The elements were already there. What Bayard needed was support for the idea and a pledge of investment to grow American manufacturing, so Chrome could expand into other categories and build a world-class brand. Rory opted for a different strategy, sticking to what had become the standard apparel industry playbook: he outsourced. Chrome products would now largely be made by factories in Asia. The days of the charmingly imperfect bags were coming to an end. "When things went overseas," Anne said, "we had three colorways only, and you had to order a million of them. It was, like, this is lame." Offshoring would minimize the role of the factory in Chico, but it saved a pile of money that could be funneled into marketing and creating a bigger output of products to grow revenues. If you wanted to scale up, that's what you did. It was how the retail game was played.

Bayard flew to China to meet with the new contract factory. That trip, and subsequent ones, made him increasingly uneasy. At Freebord, he had seen firsthand how outsourcing could cheapen the quality of a product. After the company hired a Chinese factory to make the skate trucks, the cast aluminum parts began breaking and failing on riders. The company hired a lab to do a metallurgy test, "and the test lab came back, like, 'We have no idea what the fuck this is,'" Bayard recalled. Freebord switched vendors in China, but it was an ongoing struggle to establish a first-rate supply chain. To Bayard, outsourcing was the wrong direction for Chrome. You couldn't keep a close eye on what was going on half a world away, and the bags weren't the same when they were mass-produced.

The more the production got globalized and disconnected, the more the soul got stripped away.

"You lose the character," Bayard said. "I remember at one point Rory did this dramatic unveil. He laid out a bunch of bags. He said,

'You tell me which is which.' It was immediately apparent. The thirty bags that were made in China all looked fucking completely identical, and the thirty that were made in Chico didn't. And that personality at the bag level was part of what made Chrome Chrome. You had these gritty messengers and skaters. They liked that each green bag was slightly different shades of green."

Anne Dupuis, for one, saw a conflict brewing between Bayard and Rory. "I know Bayard stirred the shit. Bayard, if he sees something and thinks it's wrong, he's going to say something. He is not someone to mince words."

Bayard believed that Chrome's customers, increasingly discerning and armed with the power of the internet and social media, would not long be fooled. Even if the changes to the bags were almost unnoticeable, people *would* notice, intuitively. About this, he had total conviction. He put the case to Rory. At some point, Chrome would cross the Rubicon. "And when you cross the Rubicon," he warned, "you're done."

⊙ ⊷⊶ ⊙

In 2010, at a meeting of Chrome's board, Bayard stood in front of Rory and the board members and argued for his vision. He spoke of the craft-brewing movement and farmers markets and how it all related to Chrome. He spoke of the renewed popularity of the heritage brands, with their rich history of being made here at home. He spoke of Americans' growing sense of loss, of a disconnectedness from how goods were produced, of a turning away from the country's identity as a nation of builders. America no longer made toys, TVs, bicycles, aspirin, tools, home appliances, computers and the chips that powered them, furniture, baseballs, baby food, light bulbs, screws, shoes, phones, kitchen cutlery, clothing, and on and on. And now America no longer made Chrome bags.

James Curleigh, a former Chrome board member who later went on to run Levi's and Gibson guitars, was present at the meeting. It was Bayard's Jerry Maguire moment: his voice intensified, his arms gestured wildly, and the little pouches of skin on his forehead puckered in fury as he lectured. "You could sense that he was trying to pinpoint not just the brand position for Chrome but saying, 'Hey, we can have a Made in America story,'" Curleigh said. Bayard wanted his bosses to take an off-ramp from the profit-making and expediency that drove corporate decision-making in the United States over the past forty years—"shareholder value," in Milton Friedman's doctrine—and to put their faith and investment behind American manufacturing, which he argued would also result in a superior product. They had to get out of China! They needed to double-down on the Chico factory and its workers! They should declare to their customers: "We're committed to American-made quality, and these bags are going to last you FOREVER!"

Recalling his piety now, Bayard laughs. "Fuckin' dude, I was committed."

Not long after the board meeting, he was fired.

Chapter 2

Flight of the Needle

America's first textile mill, in Beverly, Massachusetts, spun into operation the same year the Constitution was written, in 1787. The textile industry was the nation's founding one.

That first small factory made cloth using hand-powered, wood-frame spinning jennies. Around 1790, the jenny was replaced in American mills by the Arkwright water frame, a water-powered machine invented in England and already in use there. Now, in addition to cotton fiber, which was grown in the temperate Southern states with slave labor, textile mills needed waterpower. Cotton could be transported, but the waterpower could not, so settlements developed along the rivers and streams of New England. Newly arrived immigrants who had worked in England's mills provided skilled labor, which was often supplemented with young women and children, some younger than ten. Pawtucket, Rhode Island, where the firm of Almy & Brown installed the first Arkwright on American soil, lay along the Blackstone River. Humphreysville, Connecticut, which supplied the cloth, "made of the Wool of the pure Merinos," for the coat that President Thomas Jefferson wore on New Year's Day in 1809, sat along the Naugatuck River. Lowell, a great, teeming fortress of red brick built along the Merrimack River, was America's leading industrial city until another Massachusetts town, Fall River, surpassed it in the 1860s as the center of U.S. textile production, thanks in part to the more than thirteen hundred horsepower provided by the steep rapids of the Quequechan River. With thirty thousand looms, Fall River was known as Spindle City, and by 1876, it ranked behind only Manchester, England, in the world's production of cotton cloth.

In his book *The Run of the Mill*, a richly detailed history of New England's mill towns, Steve Dunwell argues for the very centrality of textiles to the modern capitalist nation. "The machine as ally and tyrant, the integrated factory, the corporation, the separation of management from labor, the woman as wage earner, the exploitation of a permanent factory class, the monopoly, the conglomerate, and even the American dream itself—all were developed or elaborated by this industry," Dunwell writes.

An apparel industry, of course, developed in tandem with textiles. In 1818, Henry Sands Brooks opened a clothing store on Manhattan's Lower East Side that would introduce the ready-to-wear suit to Americans and thus democratize dressing. In 1830, an English immigrant named John Rich established a woolen mill in Pennsylvania, producing early workwear like wool socks, flannel shirts, and the multipocketed railroad vest. In the 1870s, Levi Strauss, a German immigrant who ran a San Francisco dry goods store, began making denim pants reinforced with copper rivets to sell to miners and other workmen. When Seattle merchant C. C. Filson encountered prospectors passing through his city on their way to the Klondike Gold Rush, he seized the opportunity in 1897 to sell them outdoor clothing, blankets, and bags. Charles H. Beckman started making durable leather boots in 1905 for the farmers and miners of Red Wing, Minnesota. In 1909, three grandsons of an English-born weaver took over an idle woolen mill in the town of Pendleton, Oregon, and began to produce colorful blankets and apparel based on Native American patterns. (The company would later be criticized for profiting from Indigenous designs.) In 1912, an outdoorsman in Maine with the unusual name of Leon Leonwood Bean got so fed up with his shoes getting soaked while out adventuring that he invented a waterproof rubber boot. Among others, these companies—Brooks Brothers, Woolrich, Levi Strauss, Filson, Red Wing, Pendleton Woolen Mills, and L. L. Bean—established the foundation for the U.S. apparel industry and the blueprint for a distinctive, rugged style.

The French perfected the clean, elegant line and the atelier approach to making clothing. The Italians were masters of the fine handwork needed for leather goods and tailoring. What America excelled at as the apparel business scaled up and industrialized in the early twentieth century was mass-produced, good-quality, hard-wearing clothes. American workwear and sportswear, like American cars, had a tough, overbuilt quality: the copper button fly on a pair of Levi's, the waxed-cotton "tin cloth" that made Filson gear able to withstand wind, rain, and maybe even a blast of dynamite.

Much of the clothing Americans wore in the years after World War II originated in the Southeast, especially in the Carolinas, which became the new heart of the textile and apparel industries. Firms like J. P. Stevens, Dan River, Hanes, Milliken, Cannon Mills, and Burlington grew into large corporations that collectively employed hundreds of thousands of women and men across the region. Greensboro became "Jeansboro," headquarters of both Cone Mills, the weaver of denim for Levi's, and Blue Bell, the parent company of Wrangler. A single county in North Carolina—Gaston County—boasted more than a hundred textile mills, a higher concentration than anywhere else in the nation. The Wilson College of Textiles at North Carolina State, meanwhile, graduated bright young engineers who turned the region into an innovation leader in synthetic fibers like nylon.

The supply chain was remarkably efficient; it stretched but a few hundred miles: cotton could be grown on a farm in Halifax County, ginned nearby, then trucked to a spinning plant in Burlington to be turned into yarn. From there, the mills would produce "wovens" like denim and twill oxford cloth or "knits" for T-shirts, dresses, and socks. Next, finishing plants dyed the unprocessed cloth in large steel tubs of liquid dye, then bleached and preshrunk it in industrial laundry machines. Cut-and-sew factories in corrugated metal buildings in little one-stoplight towns across the South accomplished the final step: turning bolts of fabric into wearable garments.

In the thirty-year period between 1950 and 1980, the textile and apparel sector in the United States was as successful, productive, and politically powerful as it would ever be. Like the auto plant in Michigan or the farm in Iowa, the textile mill was a way of life—not only in New England and the Southeast but also in south Texas, with its denim mills, and Southern California, where a thriving garment industry had coalesced in downtown Los Angeles. Without higher education but with the technical skill that comes from doing a task repeatedly over many years, millworkers made shoes or sewed shirts or carded wool, working alongside their neighbors and family members. Wages were generally low, and the work could be dully repetitive or dangerous; some millworkers lost fingers and limbs. But a job in the mills often assured good benefits, financial stability, and the no less essential rewards of belonging to a tradition of craft and feeling pride in the creation of well-made, necessary things.

In 2001, sixty-two-year-old JoAnn Bowen, a fabric inspector at a mill in Shelby, North Carolina, conveyed to a Knight Ridder reporter just how the industry had sustained people like her for generations. Like many millworkers, Bowen had gone to work in the mills as a teenager, right out of high school. Bowen's parents had worked for the same company. Her husband, Harold, repaired looms in the same plant. "It's just been textiles," she said. "It's all I ever knowed."

◦ ◀◆▶ ◦

The textile and apparel industries did more than clothe and employ the citizenry. Taken together, they created a kind of fabric to American life. This was nowhere truer than in a mill village, the American textile industry's particular form of the company town. Many towns and cities counted a cotton mill or shirt factory among their industries, but mill villages were founded specifically to produce textiles and organized around that end, and they remained controlled by a single company or family that often ran them as fiefdoms of a sort. The ruling firm was responsible not only for the physical spaces where both the work and nonwork life of the town took place, but also for the community's social system and well-being. Woolrich, home to the eponymous Woolrich label, one of the first and most famous in American clothing, was perhaps the most quintessential and longest lived of the mill towns.

The village was established by the Rich family in the early nineteenth century, only two generations after the country's founding, in a remote and mountainous sportsman's paradise known today as the Pennsylvania Wilds. The company's formation, in 1830, predates the transcontinental railroad, the publication of *Moby-Dick*, and the statehoods of Texas and California. Woolrich beat Levi Strauss & Co. to business by more than two decades. Only Brooks Brothers, twelve years older, can claim seniority as a going concern.

Woolrich intersects with my personal history in so many ways that, to my mind, it is not a company or a place but a kind of extended family member. I grew up in those same Pennsylvania mountains, and I can trace my link back to Woolrich's original 1830 location. For a time, my mother was a dealer at an antiques store two miles from Woolrich village. The three-story redbrick building that housed the shop stood beside a mountain stream. In my early teens, during summer break, I was brought along on the days my mother worked. To stave off boredom, I spent hours outside hurling a tennis ball against the brick facade, imagining myself pitching in the big leagues. I had a sense that the building was very old—the porches that ran the length of one side appeared to sag with age—but I scarcely realized that I was pummeling the walls of Woolrich's first mill, on Little Plum Run.

I first wore Woolrich as a high school student in the early '90s, buying old flannels at the Salvation Army to dress like my grunge musician heroes. I sported a Woolrich field jacket all through college, and when I eventually wore a hole in the back where my book bag rubbed against the fabric, I patched it. Even now, there were days, especially in winter, when I was dressed in head-to-toe Woolrich, from my wool socks to my plaid trapper hat. Wearing the clothes in my Brooklyn neighborhood or out traveling in the world, I didn't feel like I was advertising a "brand." Rather, I was carrying a part of my home with me.

My family had a longstanding Black Friday tradition of making a trip to the original Woolrich outlet store in Clinton County to buy clothes for ourselves and as Christmas gifts. There was always a sense of occasion to these visits, and I especially liked to walk around the sales floor and look at the the archival Woolrich garments, which were kept inside glass cases like works of art. The center of the store was given over to a sales display of thick wool blankets, made from fabric woven across the street at the mill. Each blanket carried a tag that celebrated Woolrich's history of local production: "Our Pride Is Woven In as True Today as It Was Yesterday."

The man who built the mill I'd thrown tennis balls against was John Rich, and he embodied the restless, industrious spirit of his age. Born in 1786, in Wiltshire, England, he learned from his father, also John Rich, the trade of carding wool—that is, using a tool that resembled a wide, flat hairbrush to align the fibers in preparation for spinning. Father and son labored in the mills of West Yorkshire, in the village of Woolley. In 1811, the son sailed for America, landing in Philadelphia, where he found work in a nearby woolen factory. Some years later, Rich moved west, near present-day Lock Haven, first renting a small mill, then building his own with a business partner. The side porches that I'd assumed as a kid were sagging with age were purposely built that way to allow the water that dripped from the newly washed and hung woolen garments to run off.

Rich's wool came from his own flock of sheep and from other Pennsylvania sheep growers. In those frontier days, he traveled through the woods in a mule cart, selling his socks, breeches, and coverlets to the workmen in lumber camps. The wives of the lumberjacks bought his fabric and yarn to sew clothes for their families. When Little Plum Run proved too weak to power the growing operation, Rich acquired a three-hundred-acre parcel two miles north, through which flowed the stronger waters of Chatham Run. In 1845, after buying out his partner, he carved out a settlement with three log cabins and a larger mill. He named the community Factoryville. It was later renamed Richville before, in 1888, becoming Woolrich.

More than a century later, the village appeared hardly changed. Nestled in a shallow, forested valley well off the main highway, it felt secreted away, as in a storybook. On the approach, tall pines lined both sides of the road, forming an evergreen canopy. There was no stoplight and just one main street, Park Avenue. It passed Woolrich Community Park, the Woolrich outlet store, the post office, and, in the village center, the Woolrich Community United Methodist Church. At the church, another road branched off, veered right, and crossed a rushing stream—Chatham Run. A hundred yards from its banks were the Woolrich corporate offices and, across the road, the Woolrich woolen mill. Inside, every process required to turn raw wool into finished cloth took place.

The Woolrich mill's history and staying power were legend in fashion circles. Blankets woven there had warmed Union soldiers during the Civil War. It was also the birthplace of the buffalo-check shirt, a flannel designed as workwear in the mid-1800s and today a widely adopted classic. Indeed, the red-and-black check of buffalo plaid, likely based on a Scottish Rob Roy tartan, and so named, the story goes, because its designer tended a herd of buffalo, is one of the most recognizable patterns in the history of fashion. Nearly two decades into the twenty-first century, textile workers were still dyeing, spinning, weaving, and finishing inside the brick factory originally built in 1845.

In giving an account of the Rich clan, one wishes for a family tree blown up to poster size to keep straight the overlapping lives and recurring names. John Rich and his wife, Rachel McCloskey, the daughter of a local farmer, had fourteen children, eleven of whom survived to adulthood. John Fleming Rich, the firstborn son, joined the firm in 1864 and took over when his father died in 1870. It was he who patented the lumberjack flannel. John Fleming's firstborn son, John Rich, was the grandson of John Rich and the great-grandson of John Rich. He died in 1895, leaving his younger brother Michael Bond (M. B.) Rich to lead the firm into the twentieth century. M. B., who was raised in one of the original log homes, ran the company ably until *his* firstborn son, Robert Fleming (R. F.) Rich, took over.

What united the multiplying Rich men, besides their piercing,

hard-set eyes, was a sacrificial devotion to their company and community. John Fleming boarded millworkers upstairs in his log home
and labored beside them baling wool. M. B. Rich, in his detailed
account of the factory and village, *History of the First 100 Years in
Woolrich: 1830–1930*, praised the leadership of his relatives. "They
turned into the business all the earnings of the concern, declaring
no dividends," he wrote. "Instead, they invested and improved and
added machinery." The Riches built the community church and
served as elders in the congregation. They joined the boards of local
hospitals and colleges. R. F. Rich served two decades in Congress.
The culture of the family, and thus the community, was conservative, informed by faith, family, and work. As a strict Methodist,
M. B. Rich didn't smoke or play cards, and he claimed to have been
drunk only once, after consuming sneakily potent spruce beer at a
barn raising. When a male Rich reached sufficient maturity and experience, he was "taken into the firm," as if consecrated.

As the company and family prospered, the Riches did not move
away to more cosmopolitan towns and cities. Instead, they built
their large Victorian and Queen Anne–style homes so close to the
mill that in the summers, with the windows open, they could hear
the running looms. During the nineteenth century and well into the
twentieth, most family members were born, lived, worked, and died
in the village.

They are buried there, too. Ute Rich, who married a descendant
and lived for many years in Woolrich, gave me directions to an old
family plot. One rainy spring day, I went looking for it. The gravesite
is difficult to find now, stranded in the yard between two vinyl-
sided houses in a development called Crestmont. But the hilltop site

was once part of a farm that overlooked the original mill building where my mother sold antiques, and it contained the weather-worn headstones of John and Rachel. A newer cemetery is in the village proper. Like John and Rachel's resting place, it is located on a high point above the valley, with a direct view of the factory, as if the Riches might peer down on their business for eternity.

Mill towns held their inhabitants in a tight, paternalistic grip that could lean exploitive or benign, depending largely on the temperament of the owners. Colonel David Humphreys, the founder of Humphreysville, America's first mill town, ruled imperiously. He "instituted strict moral codes for his workers and discharged anyone who broke his rules. . . . He organized a militia company, drilling the unit himself," Steve Dunwell recounts in his history. Even his entertainments sound autocratic: Humphreys wrote plays and performed them for a captive audience of workers on holidays.

The Riches, by all accounts, were benevolent employers. When M. B. Rich died in 1930, having suffered a heart attack while driving home from the printer with copies of his company history, he left a significant sum in Woolrich stock to his employees, a final act of fidelity. The employees, in turn, voted to give back their gift to fund the construction of a community center adjoining the church. They also planted in his memory the Norway spruce trees along the main road. During the Depression, when work at the mill slowed alongside other industries, the Riches had the workers build houses in the village to keep them employed. "I never, *ever* lost a day's work because of a strike or layoff," said Ed Summerson, a thirty-seven-year employee who raised his family in one of those company houses, paying about twenty dollars a month in rent. "If one department was slow, they would find work for you someplace else. That's the way Woolrich was." He corrected himself. "That's the way the *old* Woolrich was."

Chester Pribble moved to Woolrich at the age of seven in 1931, when the Rich family hired his father as their "outside man" to farm their land surrounding the village. At ninety-five, Pribble still lived in the village when I called him in 2021, and on the phone, he enlivened the past in an amiable, commanding voice. In his account, it was clear that there was no distinction between Woolrich the company and Woolrich the community; they were indivisible. The company put in street lighting and supplied electricity to the village homes from a transformer behind the factory. The company collected residents' garbage and hauled it to its dump. Fires were put out with a company-owned fire truck, staffed by a volunteer crew of millworkers. In the early days of TV, Woolrich even became the cable provider. "They of course owned the water company," Pribble added, referring to a dam built on Chatham Run with two distribution lines, one to serve the factory and one for residents. From the company flowed the very water people bathed in and drank.

Pribble went to work for Woolrich in 1950. The president then was Ellery Tobias, who had been with the company since 1890. Pribble would go on to work for Woolrich for almost four decades, rising to become vice president of apparel manufacturing and joining the board of directors. His son and two daughters worked for Woolrich as well, making the Pribbles third-generation employees. He and his wife were lifelong members of the Woolrich community church. Pribble mentioned other families with similarly close ties— Hurlocher, Heltman, Heverly. "Those families moved to Woolrich, and they lived here most all their life."

The Riches believed that people would have more pride in the products they made if they lived in the community. It was an unwritten expectation that employees, especially senior managers, reside in the village. It was hardly a penance, for Woolrich in the mid-twentieth century was prosperous and close-knit. Children went to the village elementary school. The community park (built on land donated by the Riches) had tennis courts and a baseball diamond. In the basement of the community center was a three-lane bowling alley for league play. A little general store near the Chatham Run Bridge sold good fresh meats and cheeses and basic items, sparing families a drive to the distant shopping center. John E. Rich, a sixth-generation descendent of John Rich, married a German woman, and the couple moved to Woolrich in 1982. Ute Rich was smitten with the town from the first time she drove under Park Avenue's canopy of trees. "It just gave this impression of community," she said, remembering the Christmas ritual of company executives lighting the village tree. Summer brought outings for workers' families to an amusement park in Elysburg, Pennsylvania, owned by a family that also owned a lumber mill (hence the wooden roller coasters).

The village prospered alongside the company. From the 1950s through the 1980s, Woolrich led the booming outdoor market by many lengths. The label's chief competitors, Eddie Bauer and L. L. Bean, hired Woolrich to manufacture clothes for them. Lands' End did, too. The private-label business kept the company's ten sewing plants in steady work when Woolrich orders slowed, but for a long time, they rarely did. Woolrich grew from fewer than five hundred employees to more than two thousand nationwide. And yet the culture remained basically unchanged from the days of John Rich. The wool came from east of the Mississippi River, and the fabric was woven at the mill in Pennsylvania. Woolrich clothing was sold on a wholesale model—salesmen worked a state or a territory. Their accounts were, for the most part, mom-and-pop stores, and the families who ran Sol Marks Men's Clothing, Garrisons, and other independent dress stores kept passing the business down to the next generation, just as the Woolrich family did.

Chester Pribble, whose career exactly tracked this golden period in the history of not only Woolrich but also the apparel industry itself, called these "the happy years." "From the time I started up until when I retired"—in 1989—"the business kept growing," he said. "And every year was a better year than the previous year. So, it worked out pretty good."

● ●●●● ●

The manufacture of both fabric and clothing involves labor-intensive processes that are not easily automated. Even today, a robot is incapable of handknitting a cable sweater. What made the industry unique—the primacy of craft, the reliance on large numbers of workers—also made it vulnerable. Even more than other industries, those of textiles and apparel were responsive to, even ruthless about, labor costs in America's relentless capitalist expansion. Companies and their owners prioritized cheap labor above all else. And so, in about 1900, there came the first flight of the needle—out of New England, into the South.

By then, steam power had replaced water-driven turbines, giving new mobility to entrepreneurs and ending the Northern mills' century-long monopoly. Though the Southern mills wove coarser, less luxurious fabric, their rural white population would work for lower wages—Black workers were largely denied mill jobs until the Civil Rights Act of 1964—and millowners were hostile to the labor unions that had established themselves in the Northern factories. (This bitter hostility continued for decades; *Norma Rae*, the Oscar-winning 1979 film starring Sally Field, was based on a union-busting campaign at a J. P. Stevens plant in Roanoke Rapids, North Carolina.) As the mills abandoned New England, the textile industry there entered a period of long decline, what Dunwell calls "a lingering death," that lasted into the 1970s, after which "only the most tenacious companies survived."

And by the early 1980s, the needle was moving again—this time offshore.

Even at the industry's peak, the erosion had begun. Following World War II, the United States government, in its effort to turn a former enemy into a strategic partner in Asia, helped the Japanese build up their manufacturing base and, later, encouraged the importation of Japanese textiles by lowering the quota on them. By 1956, so much low-cost Japanese fabric was pouring into the country that the state legislatures of South Carolina and Alabama passed laws requiring merchants to post signs on their doors informing the public that they sold Japanese textiles, or garments made from them, with violators risking fines or imprisonment.

The 1960s and 1970s brought the rise of Hong Kong textile and garment factories. For American labels, the savings over domestic mills were too tempting to resist. After initially making his tailored men's clothing stateside, the fashion designer Alexander Julian was among those who transferred his operation to Hong Kong. "The first year, we made enough of my fabric—I calculated it—to go to the moon and back," Julian said. "You're buying a million yards. And the Hong Kong factories were able to give me almost exactly the same quality—at less than half the price."

Apparel manufacturers might have gone under right then had it not been for the Multifiber Arrangement (MFA). Enacted in 1974 through a bilateral agreement between the United States and other Western nations, the trade pact put quotas on the amount of goods developing countries could export to developed ones each year. In practice, it was a convoluted system—in 1984, for instance, Hong Kong was limited to precisely 123,657 dozen men's and boys' coats. Apparel brands went "quota shopping," jumping from country to country until the allotted number of pants or shirts was exhausted. But the quotas were like stones in a dam, holding the flood of imports at bay. The other backstop for American textile and apparel makers was the Berry Amendment. An obscure law passed by Congress in 1941, it stipulated that the Department of Defense had to procure essential goods, including military uniforms, from domestic sources. Government contracts to make olive drab pants, U.S. Navy peacoats, and other gear provided factories with steady work, although it was hardly sufficient to sustain a large industry.

From the eighties onward, many textile and apparel workers got the sense that the country's political and corporate elite had decided to look the other way as factory after factory closed, to quietly let a vital industry all but disappear for the supposedly greater good of free trade. This was especially felt after the passage of NAFTA, in 1993. Practically everyone working in textiles during that time points to the deal, which eliminated tariffs on products shipped between Mexico, the United States, and Canada, as a death blow. In fact, Congress instated numerous protectionist trade agreements to help the industry—LTA, GATT, ATC, and MFA I, II, and III— while legislators from apparel-making states used their power and influence to maintain them. Lawmakers won small victories, such as carve-outs for their constituencies in trade legislation, but it wasn't enough to reverse the open-trade policies promoted by both parties at the highest levels of Washington and Wall Street. Textile people discerned the unstated consensus; they spoke of their government in wounded, mistrustful terms, like soldiers abandoned on the battlefield. "Those of us who were watching were yelling and screaming," Howard Cooley, the former president of Jockey, told me. "But nobody was listening." And they weren't wrong.

Bill Brock was the U.S. trade representative under Reagan, a staunch free trader. One day in the mid-'80s, he recalled to me, a group of textile executives came to see him in Washington. The hollowing out of American industry might not have been obvious to other Americans yet, but it was already alarmingly evident to them. Tariffs were being phased out, and imports were surging by 40 percent a year. As the millowners griped to Brock about unfair competition from low-wage regions, the former congressman and senator from Tennessee had to shake his head at the way history was repeating itself. "That's how they got the textile industry out of New England, into the South!"

Brock thought back to when some textile executives had lobbied to bring more mills into his hometown of Chattanooga, in the 1950s. "What the heck do we need more dollar-an-hour labor for?" he'd reasoned. "We need the DuPonts of the world, not the cotton mills."

Historically hostile to organized labor; exploitive of women, children, minorities, and immigrants; slow to modernize, if not plain backward, the apparel and textile industry was not known for its noble conduct. And unlike the auto industry, it wasn't central to America's identity. So as one factory after another went under, the sacrifice of a whole sector of the U.S. economy to developing countries for the greater good of globalism was met in most quarters with little more than a shrug.

In truth, every party played a role in the demise. The big-box retailers, promising "everyday low prices," sold new jeans for $49.99, then $29.99, then $19.99. Ever-lower prices seemed like a neat magic trick to Americans who hadn't had a real raise in decades, but the whole system relied on exploiting impoverished workers in developing countries. Meanwhile, the big apparel brands discovered that by using cheap foreign labor and lowering quality, they could make their profits soar. Ron Frasch, the former president of Saks Fifth Avenue, once heard an apparel executive whose company hired Chinese factories boast that he'd lowered his manufacturing costs by a penny. "I said, 'Are you fucking kidding me? You get excited about a penny?'" recounted Frasch. "He said, 'We make millions of garments. That's a lot of money.'" Consumers were complicit, too—maybe more so than anyone. They wanted to save money. "They weren't going to pay more for what American production cost," said

Alexander Julian. "If you could get something as good or almost as good for half the money, why wouldn't you?"

* —— *

For a long time, Woolrich appeared insulated from the larger forces that ultimately decimated the domestic industry. But within the story of a singular American company is a cautionary tale about the difficult enterprise of making clothing here now, as Bayard Winthrop and others are attempting to.

In the early 1980s, one of Woolrich's competitors, Columbia Sportswear, opened a manufacturing facility in Asia. Columbia's president at the time, Gert Boyle, whose father had started the label in 1938, wrote of her decision in her memoir, *One Tough Mother.* Columbia's clothes had long been made by workers at its Portland, Oregon, headquarters, and as Boyle wrote, she was wary of manufacturing overseas. "I was concerned that we wouldn't be able to exert enough control over a facility that was on the other side of the world. I also thought that having the 'Made in America' label was much more preferable than one stating 'Made in China.'" Her son and business partner, Tim, had argued for the move. In the end, Boyle was persuaded. The decision would pay off handsomely—if not for Columbia's domestic factory workers, who lost their jobs, then for the Boyles and their shareholders. When the label debuted a ski jacket named the Bugaboo, in bright, eye-catching colors with a zip-out fleece liner, it was an instant hit, not least because while Woolrich and other labels priced similar jackets in the $250 to $300 range, Columbia, manufacturing at a fraction of the cost in South Korea, sold the Bugaboo for $100.

Offshoring started tentatively in the 1980s: a brand might make part of its line overseas, or buy fabric from a low-cost foreign mill while continuing to sew the garments stateside. But either out of an eagerness to boost profits or as a reluctant survival strategy, many labels, including Lands' End and L. L. Bean, moved production almost entirely offshore. Transportation costs were cheaper if a company stayed domestic, but every other input, from labor to taxes, was higher. Shoppers seemed to levy little penalty on manufacturers for abandoning America. Indeed, the big apparel brands grew bigger than ever. By the mid-1990s, offshoring had become the industry standard; to hold out was to risk your business.

To move raw materials and finished garments efficiently around the globe, apparel brands built up large production and sourcing departments. They became, in effect, logistics companies. The creative process was almost secondary. A brand made products in Mexico or Indonesia or Eastern Europe or wherever it could get the job done cheapest and best (though cheapest often trumped best). A short, rumpled, behind-the-scenes figure named Martin Trust may have shaped the modern apparel industry as much as any famous fashion designer. In 1970, Trust showed up in Hong Kong with a suitcase full of sample sweaters, seeking a factory that would make them more cheaply than the New Hampshire mill where he had previously worked. Trust imported the cut-price sweaters and sold them to U.S. clothing stores through his company, Mast Industries.

Before long, he was an expert on the global supply chain at a time when few had heard the term.

One of Mast's customers was Les Wexner, owner of the Columbus-based retail chain The Limited (and later Victoria's Secret and Abercrombie & Fitch). Wexner wanted to revolutionize fashion retail, making clothes faster and cheaper than ever before. To help accomplish that, he bought Mast Industries and kept Trust on as president. As a 1986 *New York Times* profile of Wexner revealed, Mast was The Limited's "trump card" in the new global fashion game: "Mast has interests in a dozen factories in Asia and longstanding relationships with 190 others around the world. It also coordinates global transport. . . . If fabric must be moved from China to Korea, a Mast employee is on hand to get the cloth through customs. If Columbus is desperate for a shipment of pants, a Mast executive in Hong Kong gets them on the next plane out; The Limited's merchandise fills an average of three United States–bound 747s a week."

All of this was happening as the millworkers of Woolrich, Pennsylvania, were still walking to work each morning and worshipping at church on Sundays and sleeping at night in company houses built with the beneficence of the Rich family. The first tremors came in the fall of 1990. A slumping retail market and excess inventory meant that Woolrich had few factory orders beyond December. The company whose ethos had always been to keep its workers working announced it was laying off more than half of its 2,600 employees, at least until the following spring. It was a shock to the villagers, and a sign of changing times.

More changes arrived for Woolrich in 1996, with the coming of a new president, Roswell Brayton Jr., or Roz, a sixth-generation descendant of John Rich. His solution to the offshoring dilemma was to transform Woolrich from a manufacturing business into a lifestyle brand focused on sales and marketing. Private-label orders for Lands' End and L. L. Bean had accounted for 25 percent of Woolrich's manufacturing business, and once those brands went offshore, the plants couldn't sustain themselves on Woolrich products alone. By decade's end, the company had closed its many sewing plants. In a supreme case of "if you can't beat them, join them," Woolrich began hiring low-cost factories in Asia to make some of its garments, even as the brand continued to tout its Pennsylvania-woven, made-in-America heritage.

The new Woolrich spent millions on a public-image campaign and struck licensing deals to sell watches, shoes, belts, gloves, children's clothes, and home furnishings. Eventually, you could buy a buffalo-plaid dog coat at Target and bottled water sourced from Chatham Run. The licensing agreement that would shape the company's future most profoundly was with an Italian fashion group, W. P. Lavori. It was given exclusive rights to produce and sell Woolrich clothing throughout Europe, where the label, sold as John Rich & Bros., was marketed not as humble workwear but as chic sportswear—the sort of clothing worn on the ski slopes of Chamonix and Cortina d'Ampezzo. Lavori was a modern fashion company—it didn't dirty its hands with manufacturing—and through savvy marketing and design, it turned Woolrich into a sought-after fashion brand in Europe.

In 2005, Woolrich marked its 175th anniversary with a big celebration back in the village. The tight bond between company and community had loosened since the last big anniversary seventy-five years earlier—especially in the last decade or so, with the millhouses having been sold off and trash collection and other services now being provided by private contractors. No longer was the community church the center of social life; few young people attended. The elementary school and general store had been closed. Millworkers and executives now preferred to live, shop, and play in livelier places. That included the Rich family, whose members had scattered across the country over the generations. Indeed, the company and village, like the country itself, had undergone profound changes. Woolrich had ceased its U.S. manufacturing operations altogether, except for one local sewing plant and the woolen mill. The apparel maker that had started with a mule cart in the Appalachian wilderness made very little clothing in America anymore and now had a boutique in Paris.

Andy Warlick, the CEO and chairman of North Carolina–based Parkdale Mills, one of the world's largest yarn spinners and textile manufacturers, described what it was like competing against low-cost countries, particularly China. He asked me to imagine an Olympic Games in which the athletes were treated like American manufacturers. "Let's say we're running the one-hundred-meter dash," Warlick said. "Because China's got a devalued currency, let's start them at ninety-five meters. And they're a third-world country, so now they get to start at ninety meters. The American runner has to make up those ten meters. And when our runner gets beat, we call him a loser. And we say, 'You need to train harder.' Let's say you do train harder and you're overcoming that ten meters. What happens then? Here goes the further currency devaluation. That's what it's like being an American manufacturer competing against that system."

Spinning yarn and weaving fabric is capital-intensive and more easily automated—it requires big machinery and cheap electricity—so the front end of the process wasn't as easily outsourced, and a husk of the U.S. textile industry remained. Without the decades-old quota system, however, the labor-intensive apparel sector was defenseless. Underwear, men's dress shirts, women's dresses, suits, sweaters, shoes, outerwear, socks, children's clothes—by the new millennium, all of it was made overseas. When retailers did make apparel in America, which was rare, it was usually for a limited-run project, or as a last resort—because they needed something in a rush and couldn't wait to have it shipped across the ocean by boat. Even blue jeans, the very symbol of American freedom and style, got outsourced. Companies that built their brands by marketing American culture to the world now made polos, Air Jordans, and 501s in Mexico, Honduras, India, Turkey, Indonesia, Sri Lanka, Bangladesh, China, Vietnam—anywhere but the country where they were headquartered.

This was the industry Bayard Winthrop had chosen to enter—an industry where countless others, for whom it had been a way of life, were pushed out or struggling to hang on.

Chapter 3

Silicon Valley for Socks

On a map of the country, apparel makers were now sparse dots. In Minnesota, the Faribault Mill, founded the year the Civil War ended, continued to weave wool blankets and scarves. In Pennsylvania, the descendants of John Rich still ran the oldest operating woolen mill in America, while across the state in Reading, Bills Khakis made high-waisted chinos patterned on World War II–era Army trousers. Darn Tough socks were knitted up in Vermont. Also in New England, New Balance operated four shoe factories in Massachusetts and Maine. Out in Spokane, Washington, White's Boots made handcrafted leather work boots. Designer Natalie Chanin and her workforce of home stitchers used recycled garments to produce a line of richly embroidered reconstructed shirts and dresses in Florence, Alabama, about a thousand miles, literally and figuratively, from the Manhattan fashion world where her clothes garnered acclaim. In Los Angeles, Citizens of Humanity, which owned a cut-and-sew factory and an industrial laundry, were the rare denim brand to manufacture domestically. After nearly two centuries in business, Brooks Brothers operated three facilities: a suit factory in Southwick, Massachusetts; a shirt factory in Garland, North Carolina; and a tie factory in Queens, New York. A businessman could visit the Brooks Brothers store across from Grand Central Terminal and buy a striped repp tie made just two miles away.

These and other holdouts tended to exist in places that were once major textile and apparel manufacturing centers, and where a vestige of tradition remained. Fort Payne, Alabama, was such a place.

For decades, drivers on Alabama State Route 35 passed a road sign that declared Fort Payne, a small city up near the borders of Georgia and Tennessee, in DeKalb County, the "sock capital of the world." Fort Payne claimed to be the birthplace of the cushioned sock and the leading maker of the tube sock, and for a long time, it was said that one in every eight pairs of either kind sold anywhere in the world had been knitted there. To sustain that massive output, more than a hundred hosiery mills ran twenty-four hours a day, six days a week, in three shifts, turning out millions of socks every week. For a full century, going back to the early 1900s, life in the little metropolis of fifteen thousand people revolved around sock making. There was a job in the mills for whoever wanted one.

The people of Fort Payne belonged to a long tradition: the history of socks dates to the invention of clothing itself. Cave paintings show that our early ancestors first wrapped animal skins around their feet for protection and warmth. In the eighth century BCE, the Greek poet Hesiod made what's considered the first recorded written reference to socks, describing "piloi" made from matted animal hair and worn with sandals. The Romans created the fitted sock by stitching pieces of fabric or leather together. The Vindolanda tablets, discovered in a former Roman garrison in northern England and dating from the first and second centuries CE, include a letter from someone who, not unlike a modern parent to a summer camper, has sent along some fresh socks and underpants. During the Middle Ages in Europe, socks were fused with leg coverings to become a single garment. These stockings were hand-knitted and made of silk, wool, or velvet and worn by aristocrats and wealthy men. During the 1600s and 1700s, the length of stockings moved up or down, from mid-calf to mid-thigh, with the fashion trends of the times. In the 1800s, as men moved away from stockings and breeches in favor of trousers, socks again became a distinct type of hosiery, held up with garters until the adoption of elastic. Circular knitting machines turned socks into mass-produced factory goods, most often made of cotton. The last great development in sock manufacture was the introduction in 1938 of nylon, which was blended with cotton to increase durability and elasticity.

Sockmakers came to the American South, meanwhile, the same way other apparel production did: by leaving New England in the late nineteenth century in search of cheaper labor.

In 1907, executives from a textile firm in Chattanooga were shown a hardware supply building in Fort Payne, left vacant after a brief iron mining boom in the region. The area also offered a rural female workforce willing to leave behind farm work for the better wages of factory work in town. Officially, the three-story redbrick building beside the railroad tracks was named the W. B. Davis

Hosiery Mill, after the Chattanooga executive who owned the textile firm. But folks in DeKalb County have always just called it the Big Mill.

Life in Fort Payne in the early twentieth century took shape around the Big Mill and its rhythms. A steam whistle blew in the darkness each morning at 6:15, calling the workers in. People walked down footpaths by lantern light to get to the Big Mill before the whistle blew twice. "You could look up on the side of the mountain, and it looked like the whole mountainside was lit by fireflies," said Olivia Cox, a historian with Landmarks of DeKalb County. (Cox's mother was secretary to W. B. Davis himself.) Elbert Lindsey, who grew up a block from the Big Mill, recalled to *The Birmingham News* his falling asleep as a boy to the knitting machines sounding click-clack in the night.

The Big Mill was a vertically integrated factory organized into three main departments: a knitting room, a dyehouse, and a finishing area. The knitting room was filled with rows of Banners—black cast-iron knitting machines with bobbing metal fingers, each machine standing on four spindly legs. Banners could knit tubular lengths of fabric but lacked the ability to close the toes. So in addition to the "line knitters," who operated the machines, and the "fixers," the mechanics who repaired them, a hosiery mill also employed "loopers," who ran separate machines that readied the toes for sewing, and "seamers," who sewed the toes shut. Others bleached the knitted socks and shaped them with a hot iron (known as boarding) or worked in the packaging department.

In 1939, W. B. Davis & Son patented the cushioned sock—a design that added a soft terry surface to the inside of the sock foot for extra comfort. The style was produced by the millions during World War II: from the beaches of Normandy to the jungles of the Pacific, American GIs wore cushioned socks made in Fort Payne. The Big Mill birthed a local industry that flourished in the decades following the war. Supervisors there struck out and opened mills of their own. Other townspeople formed associated businesses that specialized in a single part of the process, such as dyehouses and finishing plants, where socks were washed, bleached, boarded, and packaged on an industrial scale. Everyone wore socks, and socks wore out, so there was plenty of business to go around. Prosperity kept the competition friendly among the growing number of mills.

A cottage industry of small, independent operators sprang up to supplement the larger mills with extra knitting, inspecting, and packaging. The barrier to entry was low. A truck driver or schoolteacher could buy a couple of Banners, put them in his garage, and knit for the mills for extra money. The mills took in the unfinished goods and sewed shut the toes and dyed them. Millworkers made socks eight hours a day on the clock for W. Y. Shugart & Sons or Cooper Hosiery, then came home and spent nights freelancing for themselves. Housewives sorted and inspected socks on kitchen tables. Children were taught how to use a heat sealer, a device with a hot coil that closed the plastic bags socks were sold in, pitching in to help moms and dads. All over town, in a back bedroom, in a basement, in a garage somewhere, sock machines were clacking away.

Over time, Fort Payne became a place where a unique atmosphere of innovation and risk-taking emerged—a Silicon Valley for socks. Bob Yoe moved to town in the early 1990s to run DeSoto Mills, one of the bigger outfits. "It was the people themselves. There was a character—there is still a character—to the people in Fort Payne," Yoe told me. "There was an entrepreneurial spirit about them and a work ethic."

As a young Birmingham employment lawyer in the early '90s, Al Vreeland had a millowner for a client. During one visit to Fort Payne, Vreeland recalled, he was taken to a house in which the walls had been ripped out to put in knitting machines, a violation of every labor code he could think of. "Everything was about socks," he observed. "Even if you weren't directly in the sock industry, you supported the sock industry."

Socks provided the people of Fort Payne with economic stability. But more than that, they bonded the community together, creating what Vreeland called "commonality among the folks—a common purpose." Every August, the town celebrated Hosiery Week, a big festival with a golf tournament, softball games between the mill-workers, and a steak cookout. Making socks was a family affair: local families owned the mills, and generations of families worked inside them. In some cases, under one roof: mom in finishing, dad in knitting, brothers and sisters in the dyehouse. There was hardly a man or woman in all of DeKalb County who didn't have a connection to the hosiery business. The Locklears were no exception.

* ◁◆▷ ◁

The Locklears were Terry and Regina and their two daughters, Gina and Emily. Gina, the older of the two girls, was feisty and strong-willed. As a child, she had so much energy and passion swirling inside her that her grandmother nicknamed her Stormy. During Gina's school years, in the '90s, her parents owned and operated a sock mill just outside of town, on Airport Road. Terry and Regina weren't big players like Leman Cooper and his son, Mack, owners of Cooper Hosiery, or V. I. Prewett Jr., who in the 1950s began knitting socks with his father in a garage behind their house and from that shoestring operation built an empire of twenty-five mills, becoming Fort Payne's largest sockmaker through the late twentieth century. But they did all right for themselves. Socks bought the family a house on twenty bucolic acres and allowed Terry to put a couple of classic Corvettes in the garage. Socks paid for Emily's and Gina's college educations.

The Locklears came from sock people—Terry's mother worked as a looper at the Big Mill when he was a kid—but the family's route into the business was a roundabout one. During the '70s and '80s, Terry and Regina ran a popular local burger spot called Jack's. But Terry, who had always loved sports cars, started dabbling in the car business, going to wholesale auto auctions. He didn't really know what he was doing and kept sinking more money into the venture until things with his side hustle got so upside down that he and Regina were forced to sell the restaurant and file for bankruptcy. They lost their house, their nice wheels, everything. Flat broke, with two little girls to feed, Terry reached out to a cousin in Georgia who ran a car dealership; the cousin gave him a job. After a few years in Georgia, Terry became general manager of a dealership in Tuscaloosa, Alabama. It was an unhappy situation for everyone. Terry and Regina were living away from their families, and Terry's job was frenetically busy. He was buying and selling all the used cars, ordering the new cars, and running the service department. He kept three bottles of Mylanta in his desk to soothe the physical effects of all the stress.

One of Terry's brothers—he's the youngest of six kids—owned a sock mill in Fort Payne. One day, Terry called him up. "What do you think my chances are of getting into the sock business and making it?" he asked. His brother said, "Yeah, I think it would be good." That's all Terry needed to hear.

In 1991, when Gina was twelve, the Locklears moved back home. With $8,000 in savings, Terry and Regina bought fifteen old Banners and rented a building up on Sand Mountain, northwest of town. Calling it a mill was generous—it was a renovated cinderblock chicken coop, with barn doors on both ends. They called their new company Emi-G Knitting, after their daughters. Besides themselves, the couple had two other employees: a fixer and a knitter. Banners were considered primitive but durable, like Ford's Model T engines, and Terry and Regina would knit on the machines all day long and into the night, go home, get a little sleep, then get up the next day, get the girls ready for school, and do the whole thing again. They sold their first socks to Terry's brother Roland.

Eventually, they got in with Bubba Holland, who owned a finishing mill that took in "greige" goods—socks that had been knit but hadn't yet been bleached or dyed. Bubba could give them more business than Roland could. Terry would run the batch of unfinished socks into town in his pickup truck, and Bubba would call up Regina later to say, "I got a bad sock here." *A bad sock.* Regina thought he was being mean. But Bubba, besides doing quality control for his product, was teaching the Locklears how to knit a quality sock, with no holes or runs. Years later, that excellence would prove to be one of the things that saved them.

The Locklears were in the chicken house for just nine months, from December 1991 until summer 1992. One night, Terry was working late, alone at the mill. He'd left the door open, and five rough-looking guys walked in. They started looking around and asking questions. What was he doing? How long had he been there? How long was he planning to stay? The men hung around for half an hour, then left. Terry didn't think much of it. But one afternoon, weeks later, he heard helicopters buzzing overhead. The Hueys landed right across the road from the mill, and law enforcement officials jumped out. They were raiding a marijuana field. Terry and Regina decided the time had come to get off Sand Mountain and into a proper place in town. Regina's father, who worked at the Goodyear tire plant in Gadsden, said he would give them some money and help them build a proper mill.

Terry found a piece of land for sale on Airport Road, a light industrial area on the outskirts of town that bordered an airfield. Toiling through the heat of an Alabama summer, he and Regina's father built a four-thousand-square-foot building, a large, sturdy lean-to with a concrete foundation and framed walls. Terry and Regina and their fixer moved into the new mill with their old Banner machines and started knitting.

At the time, the family was renting the guesthouse of an estate atop a ridge on the south end of town. The property was owned by

Teddy Gentry, the bassist for the group Alabama, whose members are from Fort Payne. When Gentry sold the estate, the new owner turned out to be Bob Yoe—the textile executive who had relocated to run DeSoto Mills. Gina and Yoe's daughter became close friends, and through the girls, the families got to know each other. Terry mentioned to Yoe that he was in the hosiery business and would love to sell him some socks. Yoe told him, "Okay, make some socks, and stick them in my mailbox." Terry started stuffing two or three dozen pairs into Yoe's mailbox every few weeks.

One day, Yoe called him. "Terry," he said, "you're making good socks, but we don't have a market for them." Terry thought, *Oh well, there's another dead end.* But Yoe surprised him by saying, "Come down to my office, and let's talk sometime." Terry said he'd be there the next day.

Yoe had an MBA from the University of North Carolina at Chapel Hill. He came from a textile family—his great-grandfather was a founder of Avondale Mills, a manufacturer so big that it once consumed 20 percent of Alabama's cotton crop. Sitting in his big swivel chair, Yoe gave Terry a lesson in what he called "structural analysis," as it related to the hosiery industry.

Banners were single-feed machines—you could only load one cone of yarn on the creel—and it took about three and a half minutes for a Banner to knit a sock. That had been fine for decades, but now the bigger mills like Cooper and Prewett were switching to new, high-speed, automated machines made in Czechoslovakia—known in Fort Payne as "Anges" (pronounced like the name Angie), for the letters on the front: ANGE. These were four-feed machines, which meant that the line knitters didn't have to stop them as often to refill yarn, and they knit a sock in half the time (though they could not close the toe, so seamers were still needed). What Yoe was making Terry see was that the days when a small-time operator could buy some outdated gear and knit for the bigger mills were coming to an end.

"If you want to knit for us," Yoe told Terry, "you're going to have to get these new machines. We don't buy any stuff off Banners anymore."

One Ange cost $18,000—more than double what Terry had paid for all the knitting equipment in his first mill. But Yoe hadn't called Terry in to crush the fledgling Emi-G. Yoe had sized him up, and he saw that Terry was a hard worker who knit a quality sock. So, instead, Yoe asked how many machines Terry would need. With a banker he knew, he then arranged for Terry and Regina to get a business loan in the amount of $5 million.

Regina got physically sick at the prospect of taking on that much debt. The loan payments were $30,000 a month. But the couple was reassured by Yoe's promise. He had told them, "As long as we're making socks, you'll be able to make socks with us."

DeSoto Mills was owned by Russell Athletic. Every kid in every gym class in America wore white sport socks by Russell, and Emi-G was now making them as one of Russell's "family mills," meaning they wouldn't face production cuts even if business slowed. Soon, the Locklears had fifty employees and forty brand-new Anges in their mill, and they built a second, larger building adjoining the first to accommodate them all. "We'd get an order for a hundred thousand dozen of their bread-and-butter sock, their crew. Can you imagine that?" Terry would say years later, recalling a volume that now seemed inconceivable. The Anges ran day and night. The only time Terry's line knitters stopped them was to load new spools of yarn onto the creels. Business kept up like that for more than a decade.

● ●━━● ●

In 1998, Gina Locklear moved to Birmingham for college, where she majored in business. But by age twenty-five, only a few years out of school, she was experiencing a quarter-life crisis. Her first adult job was in ad sales, cold-calling strangers all day for a trade magazine, and she hated it so much that twice she retreated into the office bathroom and cried. After she quit the sales position, Gina went back to her college job, managing a ski-and-scuba shop. Fun, but no life's calling. Gina would lie awake at night in the bedroom of her Birmingham rental house, burning with ambition as she stared up at the ceiling and told herself, "You've got to put your energy into something that you love." Then she would ask the darkness, "What is it that I love?"

Gina next tried real estate. She went so far as to get her license and sold homes for two years, but she didn't take to that line of work, either. Then came the 2008 financial crisis and the housing crash, and no one was going to open houses anyway. When she felt especially lost in her own life, Gina sometimes thought about working with her parents in some way. Gina and her sister had practically grown up in the mill, spending hours there after school doing homework, helping their parents sort socks, and playing in the rolling bins. By high school, though, she'd become embarrassed by the family business. "Oh my God, I hated it. *Hated* it," Gina said. "When people asked what my parents did and I said we make socks, I thought it was so uncool." The college-break summer she'd spent working at Emi-G inspecting socks hadn't been more than a temporary job in her mind. But since then, she'd come to appreciate the unique culture of Fort Payne and what her parents had built.

Still, Terry and Regina had always discouraged a career in apparel manufacturing for their daughters, knowing that running a factory meant a life of instability. And by 2008, when Gina was floundering and questioning her future, so much about the hosiery industry in Fort Payne had changed that it didn't seem like there was a road back.

The trouble began in the first years of the new millennium, as if someone had flipped a switch when one century segued into the next. During that time, the Trade Act of 2002 was passed by Congress and signed into law by President George W. Bush. Among other things, the law lifted import quotas and duties for socks manufactured in twenty-four countries in the Caribbean and Central America. Under the new law, socks made from U.S.-spun yarn could be sent to Honduras or another low-cost country to have the toes sewn shut, then shipped back to America duty-free. Closing the toe had always been the most labor-intensive part of making a sock. Now manufacturers that went offshore had a competitive advantage. They saved one penny on every sock.

The senior senator from Alabama, Richard Shelby, a Republican, tried to claw back the legislation by placing a hold on the vote of another trade bill his party brought before Congress the following year. In effect, Shelby was holding his fellow lawmakers hostage in order to help Alabama's sockmakers. His efforts made him a hero in Fort Payne (and widely unpopular with Citizens Against Government Waste, an advocacy group made up of fiscal conservatives, who named Shelby "Porker of the Month"), but ultimately, Shelby couldn't reinstate the tariffs.

There were greater problems facing the sockmakers of Fort Payne. When the U.S. and other Western countries assisted China in joining the World Trade Organization in 2001, tens of millions of cheap workers were loosed upon the global economy. In China, open fields were turned into expressways, power stations, sidewalks, and streets, seemingly overnight, and factory towns specializing in garment production sprang up—Shengzhou was Necktie City, Dalang was Sweater Town, and Qiaotou was the Button Capital. Underwritten by tax breaks and land grants from the Chinese government, these new boomtowns included dormitories and mess halls for migrant workers, as well as all the necessary suppliers to support a given industry and create economies of scale. Factory owners bused in young women from rural villages, housing them in the dorms and paying them about forty cents an hour. Datang had been a rice-farming village of a thousand people as recently as the 1970s. It became Sock City. By the mid-2000s, the population had swelled to sixty thousand, and Datang's sock factories were cranking out eight billion pairs a year—a third of the world's production. The sockmakers of Fort Payne were like beachgoers staring at a coming tsunami.

In 2004, stateside sock manufacturers, led by millowners in Fort

Payne, petitioned the Bush administration to restrict imports from China. The agreement for China's WTO membership had included a clause that allowed such restrictions if a domestic industry could prove that imports had surged. It was an election year, and with the U.S. trade deficit with China already at an all-time high, the White House agreed to impose a temporary quota. For one year, U.S. imports of socks from China would be capped at an increase of 7.5 percent.

It was little more than a brief stay of execution. And in Fort Payne, the sock industry was already starting to die. In 2004, Emma Spillman, a seamer for Ben Mar Hosiery, where employees made an average of fifteen dollars an hour and had health benefits and a retirement savings plan, received her first pay cut in forty-eight years of working at the mills. In 2005, eighty-two employees of a Prewett mill lost their jobs when the company shut down its Wee Socks division. The firm cited "pricing pressure" from its customers. Walmart had found a new supplier: Hongyun Socks of Datang.

Some millowners tried to innovate their way through, buying new automated machines and trimming their workforce, but the industry's demise seemed to be on a predetermined course. The Bush administration unveiled a new bilateral treaty on trade: the Central America Free Trade Agreement, or CAFTA. The bill was an expansion of NAFTA, further eliminating trade barriers between the United States and Costa Rica, El Salvador, Guatemala, Honduras, Nicaragua, and the Dominican Republic. By now, the effects of free-trade deals were being felt in the fading fortunes of factory towns all across the country. Congress was evenly divided on CAFTA;

twenty-seven Republicans went against their party and refused to support it. Robert Aderholt, a Republican congressman from Alabama's Fourth District, which included Fort Payne, was a key holdout. In the tense hours leading up to the floor vote, Aderholt was given a letter, signed by the commerce secretary and U.S. trade representative, pledging to keep tariffs on socks in place for five years, and phase them out slowly over the next five. The bill narrowly passed the House 217–215, with Aderholt's decisive yes vote. The tariff was another temporary reprieve—one that, in the final bill, went unfulfilled.

At the peak, in the late '90s, Fort Payne's sock mills employed around eight thousand people—more than half the town's population. By 2005, the mills had shed two thousand jobs, and factories that had been in business for decades were closing or moving to Honduras.

Then, in 2007, the unthinkable happened: V. I. Prewett & Son was sold for $125 million to Gildan Activewear, a Canadian company. A slight man with a gentle, birdlike face, V. I. Prewett had been an outsize figure in Fort Payne, with a sock empire that played as significant a role as the Big Mill in the industry's evolution. He'd provided the financial backing for several of his employees to strike out on their own, and he'd shared with other millowners his cost-saving efficiencies, like sticking to one style of sock at a given plant so that the knitting machines could run continuously, without costly interruptions to change settings. Prewett began a local tradition of naming mills after family members. Lala Ellen Knitting, for instance, honored his wife. Instead of giving his children cars or houses when they came of age, Prewett gave each of them a mill.

Men who married into the family became his lieutenants. One of Prewett's three daughters married Ben Johnson, and thus Johnson Hosiery was established. David Gilbreath, who worked as an executive for Prewett Associated Mills, spoke of his former boss as if he were a titan of industry on par with Andrew Carnegie or John D. Rockefeller. "When you say he was one in a million, that's not right—he was one in ten million," Gilbreath said. "He was a brilliant engineer. He knew machinery and what it could do, and he also knew business, and when you put those two things together, you got it made."

After V. I. Prewett died of a heart attack, in 1996, his family took over the organization. Prewett Mills employed more than a thousand people and owned a million square feet of factory space in town, and it alarmed just about everyone that it was now owned by an outside company. Gildan said it had no immediate plans to cut jobs or close plants, but just two years later, in early 2009, the company did just that. Gildan announced it would phase out its U.S. sock operations by that summer. It planned to "consolidate operations in Honduras, in order to remain globally competitive."

By that point, Terry and Regina had been knitting for Russell Athletic for thirteen years. Regina, who handled the books while Terry oversaw production, had always been conservative. They'd paid off the $5 million business loan. They'd paid off the machines and the building itself. Their house was paid for, too. And still they'd managed to save some money for a rainy day. That day came in May 2008, when they were told that Russell was moving all its production offshore. Emi-G was allowed to complete the remaining orders, but there were no new ones behind them. It wasn't a total surprise. Bob Yoe had called Terry the year before to warn him that the company's production was increasingly being offshored.

Russell was the only company the Locklears knitted for at that time. Their business completely dried up. Prepared as they were, Terry and Regina barely managed to hold on to their mill. They laid off their entire workforce except for their irreplaceable production manager and plant manager, Vance Veal. Terry and Regina would come in each morning and just sit in the quiet of the mill, hoping and praying for new orders. They lived off their savings. "I was determined to keep the lights on," Terry said, because he knew if they closed the doors and turned the power off, they'd never open back up.

· ●━━● ·

It was at this uncertain moment, with her hometown reeling and her family's business on the verge of going under, that twenty-eight-year-old Gina found her life's direction. She was shopping one day at Birmingham's new Whole Foods store when she spotted some expensive designer socks on a display rack. As Gina held them in her hands, she was struck by a single thought: *we could make better socks.*

By "we," she meant her family's mill, Emi-G. In the days and weeks that followed, the idea began to form and grow inside her. The mill wasn't getting orders from sock companies, so why couldn't Gina and her parents make and sell their own brand of socks? "I was twelve when my parents started making socks," Gina said. "The realization that our family business might close made me mad. It absolutely gutted me." Fired up, she drove back to Fort Payne and pitched the idea to her parents.

After so many years of searching, the answer to her question— "What is it that I love?"—had finally come to her. Gina would return home and become a sock manufacturer. Her future was right there in her past.

Chapter 4

Bayard and Goliath

In early 2011, a few weeks after getting fired from Chrome, Bayard Winthrop reached out to Anne Dupuis, the Chrome sales executive who had shared his dismay over the cheapening of the Citizen bags. "He calls me: 'Hey, I'm making American-made apparel,'" Anne remembered. "It was that vague." He might as well have told her that he was going to push rocks uphill.

With a $25,000 investment from Don Kendall, his role model back in Greenwich, along with money he'd saved from his tech days, Bayard started his clothing company. He'd just become a father, and despite his new responsibilities, he was feeling bold. He gave the brand a name that hinted at his grand ambitions: American Giant. The name was neither overly clever nor market-tested. It was, if anything, a little out of step with modern culture in both its deliberate echoes of the era of the Greatest Generation and its overt patriotism. But Bayard meant to convey just what the name suggested: Once it was up and running, the company was going to have products sourced and manufactured in America. And it was going to be huge.

Around the same time, across the bay in Oakland, a metalworker named Roy Slaper was filling a loft workspace with antique apparel-making equipment, including a Singer sewing machine and a button-hole punch patented in 1882. Working alone, Slaper made jeans—painstakingly—with special Cone Mills–sourced denim that had been woven on antique wooden shuttle looms. These Draper looms, so named for their manufacturer, were narrow and slow: it took an hour to produce the three yards of fabric needed for a single pair of jeans, a task that modern looms could complete in about five minutes. But the result was a tight, sturdy denim with more character in the cloth and seam edges that were woven to prevent them from fraying, a style known among denim aficionados as selvedge. High-end boutiques in New York and Los Angeles sold Roy jeans for $340 a pair. This was the new, viable model for domestically crafted clothing: small-scale, handmade, and high-end, pitched at coastal hipsters with disposable income.

To Bayard, $340 jeans were "elitist and boutique." He remembered a time when good-quality, American-made clothing was sold at the local discount department store; his beloved childhood flannel had been purchased at Caldor. Others remembered, too. Brian Davis, a New York–based dealer of vintage men's clothing, could go to a thrift store, run his hand down the racks, and tell simply by touch which flannels were made in the United States before 1990 and which ones were made overseas in the years after. The older shirt "is going to be really substantial, heavyweight, and have a certain look and feel that's timeless," Davis said. "If you wanted to get that same quality today, you would have to go to a niche Japanese reproduction brand that's going to sell the same flannel for, like, $400." Bayard decided that American Giant would return to the old model. It would sell moderately priced apparel made to last. He risked his future on a kind of production that everyone said was outdated and too costly.

Anne quit Chrome and became American Giant's first employee. She was happy to be working beside Bayard again. He was an exciting boss—he lugged boxes from the storeroom with the junior staff and said "Fuck" a lot and quoted Springsteen lyrics as life wisdom. He drank coffee by the gallon (never artisanal brew, always Starbucks, which he prized for its balance of price and quality). He was direct with people and enthusiastically positive, which inspired loyalty. "Bayard has a way of making you see a bigger picture that makes life more interesting," Anne said. Of the new business, she thought, "Even to watch it fail would have been an experience."

To round out the team, Bayard brought in his childhood friend Kent Kendall as chief operating officer. Another hire, Dave Ward, had been a supply-chain manager at Adidas. Philipe Manoux was a Bay Area skater who had road tested Freebord's decks. Of the five of them, only Philipe had any design experience. He'd studied industrial design at Stanford and then worked at Apple, developing the glass for the iPhone. But for much of his career, he'd built medical devices, most recently for heart surgeries.

Philipe had just quit that job when Bayard called and asked him to sit in on a few meetings. "Why does Bayard want me to get involved in this? I don't know anything about clothes," he recalled thinking. "It was kind of weird. But I was, like, 'Sure, I've got nothing going on.'" Bayard's questionable personal style also gave him pause. "He is not a fashion person," Philipe said. "He has terrible fashion taste. That was a little bit difficult for me. Why is this guy who doesn't know anything about fashion doing this?"

Bayard had brought together this oddball group because they were people he knew and trusted, and because they themselves knew next to nothing about the clothing business. That was for the good, as far as he was concerned. For forty years, the prevailing mindset of the industry was that people wouldn't pay thirty dollars for a premium cotton T-shirt made in America. They'd sooner spend eighteen dollars for a pack of six—three dollars a shirt—made by Hanes in the Dominican Republic. That mindset had shut down the mills. That mindset had cost hundreds of thousands of jobs and gutted once-flourishing communities. It had caused a cheapening of quality. In effect, Bayard was saying, *This mindset isn't good for the country. I don't agree with it, and we're not going to bend to it and do business that way.* "The entire industry was populated by people saying no," Bayard explained. "We're trying to solve something here. Let's have a fresh perspective."

There were easier ways of making money in America in the new century. Thirty miles down the freeway in Palo Alto, smart, driven people were getting stupendously wealthy by inventing the digital future. They didn't have any made-in-the-U.S.A. hang-ups. They weren't interested in fighting the tides of history or reviving forgotten factory towns. And they did not think twice about outsourcing whatever physical components were required for their products to factories in Asia. The month that Bayard started American Giant from a coffee shop in the Castro District, Facebook reached a valuation of $65 billion. But Bayard's goal in life was not to get rich—it was to do something interesting and worthwhile. And he had a streak in his personality, a holdover from his childhood, perhaps, that made him want to stick a thumb in the eyes of Rory Fuerst and other doubters. Bayard enjoyed challenging received wisdom and taking on the role of contrarian. It came naturally to him.

Bayard rented a tiny building in the pregentrified Mission District, one room upstairs and one room at street level with a large window that looked out on a hair salon across the street called Chica Sexy. (That became the office Wi-Fi password.) The team put in a couple of desks, threw up some shelving, and stuck a table in the back for a shipping department. It was a typical start-up atmosphere: "Total excitement and energy and conviction and terror," as Bayard put it. Twice the place was broken into. The company's lone iPad was stolen. "A guy was killed right in front of our space," Bayard recalled.

Bayard's original idea was that American Giant would make modern workwear, outfitting the chefs, potters, furniture makers, and organic farmers of the new creative economy, like a contemporary version of the brand Dickies. Lacking his own factory, he would have to hire one of the surviving U.S. private-label manufacturers. First he hired the S Group, a design, innovation, and manufacturing company for apparel brands, to create a "product brand book," with inspirations, colors, fabrics, and cost breakdowns. Workwear must be utilitarian and sturdy, with abundant pockets and reinforced seams. Such clothing requires a lot of needlework—skilled labor—and very quickly the higher cost of U.S. production became evident.

"I remember flipping through the book, and Bayard and I were, like, 'Oh, shit, we're making workwear for rich people,'" Anne said. "A pair of coveralls were going to cost four hundred dollars. So we hit the reset button."

One part of the onshore supply chain that still had some meat on the bone was knitwear. As always, it came down to labor costs. Most knits—think T-shirts, leggings, jersey dresses, and socks—were made with a knitting machine in a process that was highly automated. And knits were often very simple garments that didn't require trimmings like buttons or zippers, which made them easier to cut and sew. It was still possible to manufacture knitwear in the United States and be competitive. The label American Apparel, for instance, became a billion-dollar brand selling domestically made knitwear during the early 2000s. The company flamed out amid lawsuits, controversies, and poor management, but it gave Bayard a model for how such a business could work.

One day, Anne came into the Mission office wearing a sweatshirt made by a fast-fashion retailer. Bayard started scrutinizing the hoodie. He homed in on the thin fabric, the cheap zipper, the poor construction. "He was, like, 'Stand up, stand up,'" Anne remembered. "He's, like, 'That hoodie. That is literally a *piece of shit.*'"

Bayard had already determined that four key silhouettes were the foundation of the American style canon—namely, the tee, the hoodie, the flannel shirt, and jeans. But he knew that flannel and denim were too hard to start out with, and a T-shirt wasn't substantive enough to make a real impact. "Why don't we make the best sweatshirt?" Bayard said to Anne. "Why don't we knock the hell out of it?" Remembering a popular item of clothing from his youth—thick cotton sweats made by Champion—Bayard imagined a modern version of that kind of old-school fleece. That would be the start.

Bayard put Philipe in charge of the design effort. The sweatshirt had to feel high-quality, he told him, but it couldn't cost a fortune to make or buy. It should look like those old Champion fleeces but be modern and different somehow. The fit had to be tailored but not too self-consciously fashionable. Most of all, it had to be durable. American Giant's hoodie wasn't going to fall apart after three times through the wash. It would be indestructible.

That spring, Bayard and Philipe traveled to Portland, Oregon, to the offices of the S Group, where they met with Gary Peck, the firm's founder. In a conference room dominated by a long table, they laid out fifty sweatshirts from other brands to make a market study. But Bayard and Philipe didn't yet speak the language of fashion. They couldn't tell the difference between French terry and fleece, so they struggled to explain to Peck what they wanted. After hours and hours of discussion, Peck left the room. He came back holding a garment. "Is this what you're looking for?" he asked.

The garment in question was an old sweatshirt Peck had lying around the office. It was navy, with CAL in yellow letters across the front. His younger brother had given it to him when he was a student at UC Berkeley thirty years earlier. "And the more I washed it," Peck said, "the better it became. It became heavier. It became drier. It became Old Faithful. It was just the coolest thing."

Bayard held the sweatshirt, felt its weight and quality, and declared, "That's it!"

From his decades in the apparel business, working for Nike and other brands, Peck knew his hoodie had been made on a Tompkins loopwheel machine. It took an hour to knit just ten feet of fabric on a loopwheel, its thick, round cylinder turning at a glacial twenty-four rotations per minute. U.S. mills had used the machines from the 1930s through the 1960s, and they gave the sweatshirts and T-shirts of the era a beautiful handmade quality. "The fabric is unlike anything you've ever felt," one menswear aficionado gushed in a YouTube video. "Fluffy, soft, and yet incredibly durable . . . a cottony soft more soft than any kind of cotton you've ever felt before." A few Japanese brands continued to make knitwear on loopwheels. Japanese apparel entrepreneurs had a worshipful appreciation of vintage American clothes—they had traveled across the country, scouring flea markets, thrift shops, and the deadstock of small-town department stores in search of garments from the golden era. Returning home with their haul—FiveBrother flannels, A-2 leather bomber jackets, Redline selvedge 501s woven on Draper looms—the Japanese reproduced the garments in loving detail, sometimes using the very machines that bankrupt American factories had sold off. At the Kanekichi Knitting Factory in Wakayama, master technicians coddled and refurbished the obsolete loopwheel knitters to keep them going. The Flat Head, a Japanese brand, charged ninety dollars for one T-shirt.

When Peck called around to knitting mills in the Carolinas, asking if they could replicate the old methods to make a similar product for his new client, the millowners thought he was crazy. Why not use all the efficient technology that exists today? they said.

By now, Peck had gotten caught up in Bayard's quixotic pursuit to make a brand-new sweatshirt that looked and behaved like it was decades old. He replied, "Because you can't achieve what we're trying to achieve by doing it any other way."

Everyone Peck called told him no. American Giant was a tiny, unknown company asking for a sample run of five hundred yards of fleece, enough to make about five hundred sweatshirts. Factories had minimums—the smallest quantity they would accept for a production order—and no one Peck spoke to would do such a small run. So American Giant sourced the initial fabric from India, a move that undermined Bayard's entire business philosophy. He wasn't even out of the gate with his debut product, and already he'd failed in his mission to be entirely made in America.

The compromise nagged at Bayard, and he and Peck continued to look for a domestic mill that would work with them. One day, Bayard heard about a company called Carolina Cotton Works, run by a guy named Page Ashby. Along with his grown sons, Page operated a dyeing and finishing plant in Gaffney, South Carolina, that could also develop bespoke knit fabrics. Page was an old dog in textiles, but he'd invested in the business and ran a modern, highly capable factory. Bayard flew to South Carolina to make his appeal in person, and the two men took a shine to each other. Page had been a star quarterback for NC State back in the 1960s, and he remembered the particular softness and weight—what's known in apparel making as "hand feel"—of athletic gear from the era. He liked Bayard's audacity and enthusiasm for American manufacturing. When Bayard was through pitching, Page nodded and said, "All right, we'll do the fabric for you. We'll give you a shot."

Meanwhile, upstairs in the tiny Mission office, Philipe started to work on the design of the sweatshirt. Given his background in industrial design, he came at clothing with an unconventional, anti-fashion approach. He focused on arcane aspects of construction, like the stitch spacing, the amount of elastic ribbing in the cuffs, and how smoothly the zipper zipped and how flat it lay. He incorporated several elements that no other sweatshirt on the market offered: a panel of stretchy fabric that joined the back to the front to give the garment mobility, a tailored silhouette to prevent slouchiness, and a heavy-gauge thread on all the seams for strength. To test the prototypes, Philipe would take them on his skateboard down to the coin laundromat on Folsom Street and wash them over and over to see if they held up.

Bayard, too, became obsessive about the design. Tiny details like cuff length (long enough to fold back if you wanted), drawcords (dyed to match the body fabric), and metal grommets (extra strong) consumed him. The end result was a consumer product that offered a corrective to rampant consumerism: you bought one sweatshirt, and it should last your lifetime.

Eventually, American Giant found a local factory that could sew the hoodie—SFO Apparel, five miles south in Brisbane, near the airport. SFO was owned by a Taiwanese immigrant named Peter Mou. Mou had degrees in statistics and actuarial science but fell into apparel when his sister and brother-in-law, who owned a clothing factory back in Taiwan, asked him to open a U.S.-based plant. "I tell you what, I don't enjoy this," he would say about the headaches of running a garment factory. But SFO employed more than sixty people, most of them Chinese immigrants, and Mou felt a social responsibility to his workers and their families. "Peter was just super patient with Bayard and me," Philipe recalled of his visits to the factory. "He would take me around the plant and explain exactly what each operator was doing. He would let us make, you know, five smalls, ten mediums, thirty large, and fifteen extra-large. He'd let us be annoying and accommodate us as a tiny brand."

Bayard may have approached apparel in a retro-minded way, but he'd also spent more than a decade soaking up Bay Area start-up culture. Early on, he made the critical decision to forgo brick-and-mortar stores and embrace e-commerce. American Giant would sell its products direct to consumers via a website. Instead of million-dollar print campaigns, it would run targeted ads on social media. The internet allowed Bayard to save on overhead, and those savings meant he could absorb the higher cost of producing goods in America. He would put his money into the product, not into marketing or retail stores. American Giant would be part old-school manufacturer, part tech company.

This was how American Giant managed to debut its first product without compromising on quality or charging luxury prices. Its men's hoodie, offered in four colors, was 100 percent cotton, rather than the cotton-poly blend that other brands used to cut costs, and three times thicker than most sweatshirts on the market, with a fine-textured "dry hand feel" to the fabric. It was initially priced at seventy-nine dollars—more than the Gap but on par with Levi's or J. Crew. And, most important, printed on the label were the forgotten words "Made in the U.S.A."

When the brand launched, in February 2012, the website was basic, and orders were packed and shipped from the tiny storefront. Bayard, Anne, Kent, and the others emailed everyone they knew, and a PR agency that Bayard had hired—his one extravagance—got them a few press hits. At first, ten or twelve orders a day amazed them: Who were these people, and how did they find out? Then Bayard persuaded a journalist, Farhad Manjoo, to do a feature for *Slate* on American Giant and its new business model of combining e-commerce with old-school manufacturing. The story came out that December under the headline "This Is the Greatest Hoodie Ever Made."

It went viral and changed everything.

The company's website crashed. The office line rang nonstop. The finished inventory sold out immediately. Then preorders for the next batch of hoodies sold out immediately, too. The wait to get a hoodie extended one month . . . two months . . . four months, as production backed up at SFO. Customers didn't care, said Anne: "They were, like, 'Will I get it at some point? Here—take my credit card info.'" Bayard had proved his point. You could still make quality clothing in the United States. And there was a sizable customer base willing to pay. American Giant was on the map.

Over the next five years, the company professionalized its website and marketing, left the storefront for a real office downtown, grew to forty employees, opened a few tiny retail stores (in San Francisco, New York, and Los Angeles), and expanded the line with T-shirts, women's leggings, denim, outerwear, and other items. All of it domestically made. American Giant's clothes were basic in style, of notably sturdier construction and heavier weight than much of the clothing sold by mass retailers—and at least twice the price of fast-fashion brands that manufactured overseas. The *Slate* article (and a follow-up piece by Manjoo about the long wait to get a hoodie) made American Giant a media darling. *The New York Times* wrote a feature about the company's supply chain, and the brand played off the hype to do targeted marketing on Facebook. American Giant found a following among practical, unflashy dressers who desired quality and had some extra money to spend on it. A desire to support American workers sometimes came into play as well. As a teenager, Stephen King had worked in the dyehouse of a Maine weaving mill, a place he once described as "a dingy fuckhole overhanging the polluted Androscoggin River like a workhouse in a Charles Dickens novel." King tweeted that American Giant helped him honor a personal pledge to "buy American." He even referenced the retailer in one of his novels.

In 2015, Bayard bought three sewing mills in rural North Carolina, in the towns of Middlesex, Wendell, and Princeton, and a knitting facility nearby. The mills were outdated and in bankruptcy. He put in a new HVAC system in one plant, streamlined the sewing stations for greater efficiency in the others, and saved seventy-five jobs in the process. The plants sewed T-shirts and hoodies. American Giant became what no modern apparel brand wanted to be: a manufacturer. "Levi's isn't in the manufacturing business anymore," Bayard lamented. "Levi's is in the real estate and marketing business now."

A less restless and ambitious soul might have stopped there. But in late 2017, triggered by the Proustian fashion memory of his favorite childhood shirt, Bayard turned his inexhaustible energy and focus to flannel.

The flannel shirt was, along with blue jeans and plain white tees, a classically American garment. It spoke to the rugged independence and hardworking values of the country. The origins of the fabric lay much deeper and farther afield. It likely originated during the Middle Ages in Wales, a practical response to a land abundant in both sheep and cold, wet weather. (The word *flannel* is believed to be derived from *gwlanen*, the Welsh word for wool.) But from at least the mid-nineteenth century, when the Rich family of Woolrich outfitted loggers and railroad workers in buffalo plaid, the fabric has been regarded as distinctly American, synonymous with honest physical work. If a white oxford was the office worker's default, a plaid flannel was the uniform of loggers, carpenters, lobstermen, cattle ranchers, oil field roughnecks, and all those who worked outdoors and with their hands.

My father, who worked for a natural gas company repairing huge compressor engines that pumped gas in and out of the ground, always wore quilted flannels tattered at the cuffs. Flannel's long association with the American worker does a minor magic trick: it instantly confers everyman status upon whoever wears it. Politicians put on flannel shirts to appear in touch with their voters. Folkies in the 1950s wore flannel to signal their earnest authenticity and anti-commercialism. For the same reasons, the style was later adopted by rock musicians like Neil Young and John Fogerty in the '60s, the outlaw country stars of the '70s, and the Seattle grunge bands of the '90s. (The rainy Pacific Northwest happened to have perfect flannel weather, too.) Flannel was as appealing to a farmer in Maine as to a surfer in California. You could hang it on a bedpost at night and throw it on the next morning. Mike Watt, the bassist for the punk bands Minutemen and Firehose, used to pack ten pairs of jeans and fifteen flannels on tour. He titled a Firehose album *Flyin' the Flannel* and penned an ode to his favorite shirt in *Details* magazine. "They're easy to care for. I have never ironed a flannel shirt in my life," Watt wrote, adding that "in my heart I want everyone to wear flannels and play bass guitar."

Indeed, no item of clothing may be more egalitarian or easier to pull off with a measure of style. A flannel shirt is the fashion equivalent of a Saturday morning, easy and undemanding. For all those reasons, Bayard wanted to make and sell them.

But, as he soon discovered, the simple flannel shirt is not so simple to make. It is born from a complicated union of engineering skill and artistry.

To start, harvested cotton or wool is spun into yarn. Making yarn is the first step in making nearly any kind of garment. But from there, the process for flannel is distinct. With knit material, the fabric is made first, and then whole bolts of it are dyed at once, but for flannel, each individual yarn must be dyed before it is woven into cloth. A true flannel shirt is known in the industry as a yarn-dyed woven.

There are multiple ways to dye yarn. Yarn for flannel is commonly colored through a process called package dyeing. Spools, or "packages," of yarn are lowered into a circular steel tank, and dye liquor is pumped up through the bottom and circulated in the tank. It's essential to achieve an even consistency of color throughout the yarn, and then have the colored yarn set to avoid any colorfastness issues, or bleeding. Dyeing is art as much as science; it requires a painter's eye for color matching.

Next, the dyed yarn is wound onto a large "warp" beam in preparation for weaving. Unlike the fabric for a T-shirt or sweatshirt, which is made on an automated knitting machine, the fabric for a yarn-dyed flannel shirt is made on a loom. Lengthwise (warp) yarns and crosswise (weft) yarns are woven together at a ninety-degree angle. A single warp beam may hold 3,900 strands of yarn, or "ends." And each one of those ends must be placed in a precise order so that when the beam is loaded onto the loom, the pattern that's woven matches what was designed. A flannel shirt might have as many as ten different colors, which is what gives it its intricate, patterned look. But get a few stray red yarns running through a black square in a buffalo plaid, and the fabric is useless. Warping a flannel shirt is like assembling a three-thousand-piece jigsaw puzzle made of yarn.

And as anyone knows, what really makes flannel flannel is its soft texture. That characteristic cozy fuzz is created after the fabric is woven, through a process called napping. Imagine big rollers with wire hooks that stick up. The hooks catch the yarn and rough it up, raising some of the fibers. That's what gives flannel its fuzzy surface, and its softness. Napping, like dyeing, requires an aesthetic sensitivity: If the napping machine is set too tight, the fabric will come out with holes in it. If it is set too loose, it will come out with no hair, rough as sandpaper. John Bakane, the former CEO of Cone Mills, which in the 1970s was the world leader in cotton flannel production, described flannel to me as "a very complex product from start to finish," and called the workers who ran the napping machines "artistes."

After the fabric is napped, it goes through another finishing process called preshrinking, in which it gets compressed by a roller to stabilize the dimensions. Finally, the dyed, woven, napped, and finished fabric is sent to the apparel factory, where it is cut and sewn into shirts. A final complication: the sleeves, collar, pockets, and body must be assembled in such a way that the plaid pattern aligns. (Plaid and flannel, incidentally, are not the same thing. Plaid refers to a pattern of crisscrossing horizontal and vertical bands in various colors, traditionally worn in the Scottish Highlands, where it's called tartan, while flannel is a type of fabric. But since nearly all flannel shirts have a plaid pattern, the terms have become largely synonymous.)

Even when the American industry was at its peak, making flannel apparel was difficult. Each of the steps demanded great expertise.

And when Bayard began calling around to people he knew in the apparel industry looking for advice, he was told that flannel was no longer made onshore. L. L. Bean, Woolrich, Eddie Bauer, Pendleton, Ralph Lauren—all the brands that traditionally sold flannels—now made them overseas, which struck Bayard as strange. All that trouble, all the human exploitation and environmental harm that came with outsourcing to factories in developing countries, undermined the message of simplicity, the kind of rough idealism, that the shirt itself conveyed.

No one Bayard talked to could even tell him when a flannel shirt had last been made stateside. The best guess was sometime in the '90s. Flannel, they said, was a lost craft.

● ◀▶● ◀

Who had made the last American flannel shirt? And why had they stopped? When I dug deeper into this question, all roads seemed to lead to an ex-hippie from New England named Mark Baker. In the early 1980s, following a brief stint as a roadie for a jazz fusion band and several years working for an ad agency in Boston, Baker moved to East Barre, Vermont, and started a T-shirt company, Ad Art America. He sourced the T-shirts in the United States, then screen printed them for the college ski trade, coming up with the slogans himself:

"No Guts, No Glory. No Falls, No Balls." For a decade, Baker tried to come up with the next yellow smiley face—the graphic symbol or saying that would catch on and sell a million T-shirts.

With the onset of the Gulf War, he thought he'd found it. Baker designed a concert tee: "Saddam Hussein Middle East Tour 1991" it read, overlaid with a giant stamp that said CANCELED DUE TO DESERT STORM. In tiny East Barre, Baker sold two thousand shirts within a week. Encouraged, he paid $8,000 to rent a booth at an apparel trade show in Atlantic City, where buyers from JCPenney and other big retailers made their purchase orders. But before the show took place, a cease-fire was brokered, the war was over, and his bestseller was instantly démodé.

Baker scrambled to come up with another product to bring to New Jersey. He hit upon the idea of flannel sportswear. Traditionally, flannel was used for pajamas and hunting clothes, but Baker's impulse took it in a different direction. "I invented the first pair of flannel lounge pants," he told me proudly. "Meant to be worn outside by college students hanging around."

It was summer in Atlantic City. Standing in his booth promoting flannel leisurewear, Baker was openly mocked. "I had never been insulted more in my life. *What are you doing here?* Must've been asked that a hundred times."

But by day two, he'd logged a few orders. And out of the flop was born a new business: the Vermont Flannel Company. Flannel jam shorts. Flannel underwear. Flannel shirts. Flannel everything!

Like Woolrich, Levi's, and other brands that sold cotton flannel shirts back then, Baker sourced his fabric from Cone Mills in North Carolina, working with the company to create flannel to his specifications—a bit heavier, tightly woven, and double-brushed on the inside to be luxuriously soft. A team of stitchers, older women who'd learned to sew from their mothers or in home ec, made the garments in a small Vermont factory.

Baker's decision to manufacture in the United States was motivated less by strongly held principles than by convenience. As a small business owner, he found it easier to deal with a mill in the same time zone than one halfway across the world. And back in the '90s, there were still plenty of mills around to hire. But the longer Baker stayed in business, the longer he competed against bigger brands that outsourced, the more his position of convenience hardened into a conviction.

Once, Baker claimed, he saw a flannel pullover at JCPenney that looked exactly like one of his designs, and it was selling for half the price. His direct competitor in New England, L. L. Bean, played up its local heritage but, by the '90s, was making flannels in Cambodia and El Salvador. L. L. Bean could undercut Vermont Flannel on the price of a shirt right in Baker's backyard. Another time, Baker angrily recalled, Coors approached him about making flannel shorts for a beer promotion. "I told them they would cost seven dollars each to produce, and that since we're a small company, we would need to be prepaid. They came back with, 'We can get these shorts for two-fifty from China.' This from a company that promotes its Colorado water!" In the end, Baker resolved to make clothing in America out of spite. "I was so pissed off that I wanted to distinguish myself," he said. "'*No*, this is *not* made in China.'"

By the late '90s, the Vermont Flannel Company may have already been the lone brand selling American-made flannel shirts.

Ralph Lauren, Woolrich, Eddie Bauer, and other retailers had long been manufacturing in Asia and elsewhere. Even if a shirt was sewn domestically and advertised as "made in the U.S.A.," the tag would often note in small print that it was crafted "of imported material." L. L. Bean, for instance, purchased fabric from mills in Portugal, a current leader in flannel production. Pendleton still wove fabric at its Oregon mill, but the sewing was outsourced to Asia.

In early 1999, Baker received a fax that upended his business. He was informed by Cone Mills that it was discontinuing production of its yarn-dyed wovens by that spring. Vermont Flannel purchased a hundred thousand yards of fabric each year from the mill—an insignificant order to Cone but sizable enough for Baker to expect a little advance warning. He had built his entire business around Cone's fabric. He was panicked—and angry—at losing his only supplier.

As Baker tells it, he got in his beat-up Plymouth station wagon and drove eight hundred miles to Greensboro to chew someone's ear. At the time, Cone was one of the major textile companies in the world; its corporate headquarters featured a long, winding driveway and landscaped grounds with a fountain. Baker marched into the lobby and asked to see John Bakane, the CEO. Bakane's secretary asked if Baker had an appointment. Baker said, "No, but I have a station wagon with seats that fold down and a sleeping bag. You can tell him that I just got two weeks' notice that he's going to ruin my business. So I'd like to talk to him."

To his credit, Bakane did meet with Baker that day. He apologized for the abrupt notice and referred Baker to another mill in Texas that could weave flannel for him. Twenty years later, Bakane had no memory of the meeting but said it had the ring of truth.

Cone had referred its customers at the time to a competitor in yarn-dyed wovens: Mission Valley Textiles in New Braunfels.

Bakane was having his own problems. When he'd joined Cone Mills in the mid-1970s, the company employed seventeen thousand people at more than twenty plants, including its White Oak mill, the holy temple of selvedge denim with its Draper looms. Cone's Revolution Mill in Greensboro was a city unto itself—more than half a million square feet spread across a complex of twelve buildings, with a yarn mill, a weaving mill, a dyehouse, a finishing plant, warehouses, and offices. But by the time Bakane assumed the top job, in 1998, Cone was getting killed by Asian imports. The apparel manufacturers and fashion brands that were Cone's longtime customers for fabric were either going out of business or moving overseas. There was nobody left to sell to. Bakane's role became more like triage. He had the thankless task of offshoring a great American company. "Under my watch," Bakane told me, "we started Cone Denim Jiaxing in Jiaxing, China. We took all manufacturing except for a very small plant, White Oak, offshore." (White Oak was eventually closed in 2017.)

One of the casualties was Cone's Salisbury, North Carolina, plant, which made chamois and flannel—including for the Vermont Flannel Company. Cone had already shut down its main engine of cotton flannel production, the Revolution Mill, in 1982, following a string of costly incidents involving flannel sleepwear. Careless smokers would drop a stray ash on themselves or their children, catch their flannel pajamas or bedding on fire, and file lawsuits against the company. That had left Salisbury as the last bastion of flannel. When Salisbury was closed, it left nothing.

Determined to keep his production in America, Baker called Mission Valley. The company, which had been founded in 1921, supplied him with flannel until it, too, went out of business a few years later.

Baker was out of options. He reluctantly began sourcing flannel in Portugal, like his archrival, L. L. Bean. He continued to pay stitchers in Vermont to sew the clothes. But under U.S. Commerce Department regulations, he couldn't label his flannel shirts "Made in America," because the material was imported. Instead, they were "Handcrafted in America."

● ●●●● ◉

Bayard didn't want to source flannel from abroad. And he certainly didn't want to do what many retail brands do today to save time and money—make an ersatz version of flannel, in effect stamping a plaid pattern onto a roll of undyed fabric. Not surprisingly, he wouldn't consider making anything but yarn-dyed flannel the way it had been made traditionally, no shortcuts. He wanted to make your grandfather's flannel shirt.

Bayard had staked his career on choosing to do the thing that people said was not possible—manufacturing mid-priced clothing in America—and then doing it. The notion that the United States really had lost the ability to make a simple flannel shirt mystified him. More than that, it pissed him off. After half a decade in business, he felt he had the experience and the industry relationships to take on his holy grail. And he wasn't taking no for an answer.

No one else inside or outside the company was initially as committed as Bayard to this quest. Pete Dinh, American Giant's chief financial officer, worried that the idea was folly. Within the company, Pete was the guardrail to Bayard's careening car. "You have to stand up a supply chain from scratch," he told Bayard. "It's going to require a huge amount of attention from the company. You weigh that against how much sales can you drive?" After considering the pros and cons, Pete concluded, "I wouldn't do it."

The manufacturing experts Bayard spoke to warned him that, because flannel hadn't been made in America in years, the men and women who once knew how to do it were either retired or dead. They emphasized, over and over, that making a woven shirt like flannel was far more complicated than making a knit hoodie or tee. "We kept hearing, 'You can do all these other things here, maybe,'" Bayard recalled. "'But not flannel. Flannel is gone.'"

Whenever Bayard heard this, his eyes would narrow, his face would redden, and the lines on his forehead would pucker up in indignation. He would practically yell, "*Why* isn't it possible? The technical ability has left? The machinery has left? It costs too much? This is *bullshit!*"

He'd hold up his iPhone to whomever he was talking with and say, "You've got phones capable of doing all these things; you've got driverless cars. Forty years ago, we were able to make great clothes here, sold at a price that made sense to mainstream consumers, that were of the finest quality. We've lost that capability in forty years?" The question would hang in the air. "I'm not going to accept that answer!" he'd roar.

To resurrect American flannel now, Bayard would need to find partners up and down the supply chain to spin, dye, warp, weave, nap, and sew the shirts. Solving for the first step was easy enough—the United States remains a world leader in growing cotton, thanks largely to generous government subsidies for farmers. Bayard would use homegrown cotton spun into yarn by North Carolina's Parkdale Mills. But the labor-intensive wovens side of the business had been eviscerated as a result of outsourcing. Once Bayard had those spools of yarn, the rest of the process promised to be a trial.

He got started in January 2018, setting himself a tight deadline: the first shirts had to be finished by November, ten months away, to coincide with the holiday season, after which no one bought flannel until the following fall.

It was around this time that I'd first got wind of Bayard's quest. We met at a restaurant in lower Manhattan, where I watched him wave his iPhone over the table incredulously as he described the plight of the craft of flannel making. Viewed one way, Bayard's aim was very basic—make a shirt. But I was struck by the way the project raised larger questions about the past and future of America. About how much of the country's manufacturing sector had been shipped offshore over the past forty years, and how much could be saved or brought back. And whether Americans felt that cheap Chinese-made jeans and flat-screen TVs were worth the trade-off. What would it take for other businesspeople, whether CEOs of big companies or smaller-scale makers or entrepreneurs, to join him and his hardy fellow travelers in making their products in America again? Or was Bayard a lone figure shouting into the void? Garment by garment, he was trying to build back the supply chain. With flannel, he was upping the challenge for himself and daring his competitors.

Indeed, for Bayard to attempt American flannel in 2018 was a little like President Kennedy declaring in 1962, "We choose to go to the moon." Pulling it off would require a huge investment of resources and energy, a team of experts working for a common cause, and a few miracles. At American Giant, the mission was there; every employee had signed on to it by virtue of deciding to work for the company. "The dream here, as I understand it," said the label's head of product development, Tam Ravenhill, "is to make sure that we don't lose all the work and ingenuity and the ability to make things in the U.S. That isn't going to happen because American Giant exists. It's going to happen because people see American Giant doing it, and they join in."

Chapter 5

Heritage Land

The enthusiasm and determination of a given entrepreneur was only half the equation. To succeed, a business needed customers—and customers, like clothing itself, could be created. The heritage trend that revived historic apparel labels like Woolrich and Filson, and helped propel new brands like American Giant, did not arise spontaneously; it emerged from certain social and economic factors. And it was not only chronicled and debated but also to a great degree birthed and promoted by a men's style blog called *A Continuous Lean*, or *ACL*. And *ACL* was really just one person: Michael Williams.

Williams had grown up in blue-collar Ohio, in a suburb east of Cleveland called Wickliffe. The families in his town lived in modest bungalows with well-kept lawns, and the parents worked at an injection molding plant or in machine shops, or maybe they owned those kinds of small businesses. Williams's father ran a landscaping business in the summers and in the winters plowed snow around town and sold firewood to homeowners in wealthy enclaves like Shaker Heights. When Williams turned fourteen, his father took him to buy his first pair of Red Wing work boots. He worked for his dad on weekends and during summer vacation all through high school—that he would do so was understood.

As a kid, Williams was fascinated by the heavy industry that had made his hometown. "You see steel mills, and they're the most impressive places," he said. "I was always awed by it." But by the time he was coming up in the '80s and early '90s, the factories were closing, the city was near bankruptcy, and Cleveland had become a national punch line for late-night comedians. Like many natives of the Rust Belt, Williams developed a chip on his shoulder. He wondered why his region was in decline and why the country's leaders weren't doing anything to stop it. He knew that something in American life had gone profoundly wrong, but he had only a vague sense of the larger forces at work. And like a lot of other kids from such places, he moved away. He graduated in 2001 from Ohio University, where he'd studied retail, and "just instantly moved to New York. All the jobs were in New York. I had ten grand from selling my car. I was, like, 'I have ten thousand dollars' worth of time to make it.'"

He landed a job as an assistant at a fashion PR firm, and after six months he moved to a bigger agency that represented Abercrombie & Fitch and Sean John, the rapper Sean Combs's label. In 2007, Williams and a colleague, Ali Paul, started their own boutique agency, Paul + Williams. One day, he visited a factory in Chelsea called Bentley Cravats. The factory made ties for one of his new accounts—J. Press, the preppy clothier founded on the Yale campus in 1902. On the ground floor was a very nice gallery selling work by blue-chip artists. Taking the elevator up several floors, however, Williams was transported to another time. The factory was a messy space with fabric scraps everywhere and rolling carts piled with finished ties. Workers stood at long cutting tables carving up the cloth that a dozen or so sewers would fashion into more ties. "It felt like I was seeing something rare that most New Yorkers don't know even exists," Williams said.

Tagging along with Mark McNairy, a young designer for J. Press (and later Woolrich), Williams began visiting the city's other garment factories, like Primo Coat in Queens and Martin Greenfield Clothiers and Hertling USA in Brooklyn. Martin Greenfield was one of the top producers of handmade tailored suiting in America, with a client list that included Paul Newman and Michael Bloomberg. Founded in 1925 by Morris Hertling and run since the '40s by Morris's son Julian, known as Julie, Hertling USA made beautiful trousers for J. Press, Paul Stuart, and other menswear labels. But nobody outside the industry had ever heard of it. These family-run factories were a holdover from the days when New York had been a leading garment center, and they reminded Williams of Ohio, rekindling his interest in the workings of industry. "It was very rare to find stuff still made in the U.S., and I wondered, *Why?* And, more specifically, *How are the people who are still doing it, doing it?*" Williams wanted to champion and promote this lost breed of craftspeople. "I had all this stuff inside of me that I wanted to say and no outlet for it in my job. I was, like, 'I should start a blog.'"

On Thanksgiving Day in 1985, as Americans sat down to gorge on food and football, they saw a TV commercial featuring Bob Hope and other celebrities asking them to buy clothing with the "Made in the U.S.A." label. To do so was to "tell all the world America matters, America matters, America matters to *you*," as the jingle went. The spots were part of a new campaign by the Crafted with Pride in U.S.A. Council, a group made up of manufacturers and garment workers' unions led by Roger Milliken, the chief executive of Milliken & Company, his family's South Carolina textile business. The campaign echoed one from the mid-1970s, when the International Ladies' Garment Workers' Union, or the ILGWU, had urged shoppers in a catchy singsong to "always look for the union label." Back then, imports were a growing problem, accounting for about 30 percent of the clothing Americans bought. By the mid-1980s, imports had soared to nearly 50 percent, and an estimated three hundred thousand textile and apparel jobs had been lost in the first half of the decade alone—a full-blown crisis. At the same time, the Big Three in Detroit were getting bested by Japanese carmakers, and California tuna packers were losing market share to Thailand. The country was starting to see the profound effects of globalization.

In a way, the Bob Hope ads were a sentimental appeal, relying on pocketbook patriotism. In marketing surveys conducted by Crafted with Pride, shoppers said they preferred products made in their homeland—provided they could purchase them at comparable prices to imports. The ads, then, were a call to national unity and action: Americans should buy jeans and dresses just as they'd once planted victory gardens during World War II. But trade wars didn't feel as immediate as armed conflict to most consumers, and clothes made onshore were already getting hard to find. Taking up the challenge of the ad campaign, a reporter for the *Orlando Sentinel* went shopping for clothes with the "Made in the U.S.A." label. "It is a task that requires training and sophistication," he wrote, "like hunting for edible mushrooms."

The campaign continued for several years and ultimately cost $85 million, with a growing number of celebrities joining the cause, but despite the genial pleadings of Sammy Davis Jr., Ted Danson, Don Johnson, Loretta Swit, Billy Dee Williams, and Hope himself, Americans continued to buy foreign-made clothing by a wide margin. By 1990, imports had grown to 60 percent of all apparel sold, and job losses were nearing six hundred thousand. That year, Crafted with Pride dropped the celebrities and changed its tone. Americans didn't need a gentle reminder to support their own industries and neighbors. What they really needed was to be shown, directly and starkly, the cause and effect of their spending habits. In a new ad spot, men, women, and children gathered at a pier to watch a crate of imported clothing being unloaded while a narrator gravely intoned that America was losing its apparel industry. "And the worst part is," said the narrator, "we're doing this to ourselves."

As Dana Frank points out in *Buy American*, a history of economic nationalism, it was an American-made campaign that gave birth to the United States: the colonists who organized the Boston Tea Party were rejecting imported goods from Britain to assert economic independence. Down through the years, textiles and apparel have tended to play a central role in such movements. Nine years before the Tea Party, in 1764, a group of Boston merchants pledged to give up lace, ruffles, and other ostentatious cloth made in England, and soon many colonists, including George Washington and Thomas Jefferson, were dressing in "homespun," the humble term given to cloth produced domestically. A reaction against foreign imports often arises in times of economic and social distress at home, Frank observes. In 1932, for instance, the newspaper baron William Randolph Hearst launched a Buy American campaign in an editorial in Hearst newspapers. Although he presented the idea as a solution to the Great Depression, Frank notes that he may have been motivated more by his isolationist politics. More than 250,000 people signed the accompanying pledge, and the campaign had enormous impact. The campaigns by the ILGWU and later Crafted with Pride similarly grew out of a jittery period for workers. "All over the country during the 1970s, '80s, and '90s," Frank writes, "ordinary people were worried about unemployment, increased economic inequality, and the future of the United States in a rapidly globalizing economy."

At some moments of economic anxiety, Americans have responded to the threat of imports with what Frank calls an "import panic attack." In the summer of 1985, the Coca-Cola Company introduced a line of clothing produced mostly in Macao and Hong Kong. For textile makers in the South, where Coke was considered as life-giving as water, this was a betrayal worse than the "New Coke" formula the company had introduced earlier that year. "I once had a dog who bit my hand when I fed him," the president of a North Carolina fabric firm wrote in a letter to the company. "I got rid of the dog and we will get rid of Coca-Cola Co. in our plants if it continues to bite our hands." Some plants did yank Coke from their vending machines. The story of the protest got picked up by newspapers across the country, and the president of a bottling company with rights to the Coke franchise in the Carolinas and southern Virginia, where half a million people still worked in textiles, had to step in to broker a truce. At the American Yarn Spinners Association office in Charlotte, a repentant Coke executive met an angry group of textile leaders and emerged from the meeting chastened. By the following summer, Coca-Cola clothing was being made in U.S. factories, and break rooms across the South were again stocked with Coke.

A generation later, in the years after the financial crisis, Americans showed the same righteous anger when, ahead of the 2012 Summer Olympics in London, it was revealed that Ralph Lauren, the official outfitter for Team USA, had made the athletes' opening ceremony uniforms in China. For many, this outsourcing illustrated America's woeful dependence on imports. "The Italians would never have their uniforms made in China, they would make them in Italy," Galina Sobolev, an L.A. designer, told the *Los Angeles Times*. Washington lawmakers especially displayed outrage, perhaps because it was an election year. (Ralph Lauren had made uniforms for the 2008 and 2010 games abroad as well, to no apparent concern.) House Speaker John Boehner, a Republican, publicly scolded the U.S. Olympic Committee, while Senate Majority Leader Harry Reid, a Democrat, called for burning every uniform and starting over. The controversy was such a public-relations disaster for Ralph Lauren that for the 2014 Winter Games in Sochi, the label promised to make all the clothes in the United States, for the athletes and Olympics retail products, which required building a supply chain practically from scratch. (The company had closed its last Polo menswear factory, in Massachusetts, in 1994.)

Actual consumer behavior is different from performative outrage, however, and Americans, broadly speaking, have proved to be fickle consumers, whatever they may say or pledge. The unbounded freedoms we cherish apparently extend to the goods we buy and the merchants we patronize. In 1771, Thomas Jefferson wrote his agent in London to request a personal shipment of "some shoes and other prohibited articles," even as he touted the virtues of homespun. In my own dresser drawer, American Giant tees mingled with Hanes tees made in the Dominican Republic and American Eagle underwear from Vietnam, even as I immersed myself in the world of American-made clothes. The contradictions could reach absurd levels. I once came across a vintage Ruff Hewn flannel shirt with "True American Wear" written on the label—and underneath it, "Made in Hong Kong."

Ultimately, what got people to buy American wasn't making it patriotic; the lever was making it fashionable. Tapping into deeply held nostalgia for craftsmanship and good value surfaced what was so appealing about domestically produced goods, instead of just shaming or lecturing consumers into purchasing them. This was the chord that Michael Williams managed to strike. By amplifying the outposts of quality domestic manufacturing that remained and giving them a kind of cachet through his blog, Williams created openings not just for survivors to thrive but for new entrepreneurs to get a footing. As one *ACL* reader commented, "Made in the U.S.A." was the new cool.

As a reminder of what had been lost—and what still remained—
Williams began giving his readers virtual factory tours. He'd visit a
shoe workshop or denim mill, then post photos of these rare folks
who were engaged in making things. He made dusty old factories
seem like the most amazing places. The American List he compiled
("A guide to great things still made in the U.S.A.") included heritage labels like Alden Shoe Company, Pendleton Woolen Mills, and
Hickey Freeman but also a new generation of brands like Rag &
Bone, Imogene + Willie, Raleigh Denim, Buck Mason, and Steven
Alan. The founders of these companies saw the virtues of local
manufacturing and, as with American Giant, had built their businesses on an old-school model of quality.

At the outset, Williams didn't expect many people to read his
blog, given that so few made any special effort to buy in their own
backyard. But the personal, ongoing nature of a blog not only allowed him to go deeper than a magazine article in his exploration of
the topic, it also allowed him to create a community around the
subject. He covered menswear the way ESPN covered the NFL
draft—that is, authoritatively and exhaustively. He was an enthusiastic fan and guide, and like all successful bloggers, he had a com-
pelling point of view—in his case, about what constituted good
value, high quality, and responsible consumption.

Williams could be prickly. He didn't hesitate to call out brands for
perceived infractions. When Carhartt partnered with the designer
Adam Kimmel on a collection, Williams wrote critically of the
company for not making any of the clothes stateside. But Williams

wasn't a purist: he didn't think *everything* had to be made domestically; that was no longer possible. He argued that brands should give customers the option, that "everything doesn't have to be imported or nothing."

Williams wanted clothes to have history and meaning, rather than being meaningless throwaway purchases. He became a leading proponent of a philosophy known as "Buy Quality, Buy Once." The idea was that rather than purchase lots of cheap, disposable products, people should spend more on a few well-made items and use them for years, in effect reducing their consumption. (Someone who shared this view, incidentally, was Tony Bennett. "The only thing that lasts is quality—suits, music, people," the singer once said in an interview. "It's all the same. My suits are very expensive but they never go out of fashion, and I can keep them for up to two decades.")

Williams's blog turned out to be the perfect meeting of medium and moment, serendipitously tapping into a deep well of feeling. His argument for timeless quality resonated with the young urban professionals and fashion addicts who made up the most devout followers of the heritage movement, as well as with older readers who remembered a time when America's factories hummed and stores sold U.S.-made goods.

ACL's comments section became a lively forum for debating the finer style points of crepe soles versus lug soles, but just as often, it was a place to sound off about the hypocrisy of companies that pledged allegiance to the flag but manufactured offshore. "As the owner of a retail store that has sold Carhartt since 1979 . . . I remember when it was all made in U.S.A.," wrote one commenter when

Williams covered a Made in the U.S.A. capsule collection released by the workwear label. Another added: "Now we struggle to find work clothing made in the U.S.A. Sad. Carhartt come home. And bring the rest of the economy with you, please." Advocates of outsourcing liked to point to all the good corporate jobs that remained, even if the factories were gone. But it had been the factory that, for nearly two centuries, had given America its identity as a country that produced things, and no number of office jobs in New York or Palo Alto was going to restore that. Not when compared with the country's manufacturing past. Speaking to *Women's Wear Daily*, Williams gave voice to the sentiment that animated him: "I don't want to live in a country that doesn't know how to make anything."

To be sure, as the journalist Robert Armstrong pointed out in the *Financial Times*, the obsession with quality could be a rationale for "desperate style addicts" aching to justify another $800 cashmere sweater as an investment piece. And Williams *was* a style addict; he collected fine watches and owned Red Wings in every color. On his blog, he seemed to battle with his own material desires; he repeatedly reminded his readers and himself that you couldn't buy happiness with *stuff*.

There were some who thought that telling people to invest in expensive things seemed impractical if not elitist—wasn't *artisanal* just another word for *luxury?* America's pinched working and middle classes bought cheap stuff at big-box stores not always by choice but out of economic necessity. And while General Motors and Ford did brisk business selling $60,000 pickup trucks, many Americans had evidently decided that premium American-made clothing was not something on which to spend their limited disposable income.

Williams understood that person. His father *was* that person. "He wants Carhartt to be all made in the U.S.A, doesn't want any non-U.S. shit in the line," he said, "but then he won't buy it, because it's too expensive."

But Williams truly believed that buying $300 Red Wing 875 boots made more practical sense in the long run than buying $40 boots at Walmart. The Walmart boots would be shot after a year of heavy use, whereas Red Wing has a program that let customers send their boots back to the factory to be refurbished, extending the life span by years. Buying domestically, he maintained, was a good economic proposition all around. "You're investing in your community, and you're buying something that is probably well-made. Stuff that's still made here has survived for a reason."

And by the early 2010s, a new zone had opened up, a middle ground of quality at higher but not exorbitant prices. Bayard Winthrop and Gina Locklear were part of this trend. So was Todd Snyder, who during his days at J. Crew partnered with the shoemakers Red Wing and Alden, bringing handmade products to the mass retailer. "Every factory I've walked through, it always hits me: this stuff is too cheap," Snyder told me. "After you see the amount of labor and the number of hands that have touched it, you're, like, 'And this only cost $300?' That's why I've taken it upon myself to help tell that story. Because I think my customer likes quality and likes knowing where their stuff is made." Maybe a person living paycheck to paycheck wouldn't buy from American Giant, Steven Alan, Buck Mason, and other labels like it, but someone with a little more means might.

As his readership and influence grew, Williams found that he could help launch new businesses. He noticed a guy selling handmade leather footballs on Etsy, wrote about him, and blew up the guy's sales. The founders of Noble Denim credited his blog as an inspiration to start their apparel company. In turn, Williams wrote about the fledgling brand and others, giving them a boost.

As *ACL*'s reach expanded, Williams saw that he could use the platform to not only inspire and support new businesses but also help save established ones. J. W. Hulme was a one-hundred-year-old bagmaker in St. Paul that produced canvas hunting bags for Orvis and leather goods under its own name. By 2008, the brand was on the verge of bankruptcy. Steven Alan read the story Williams had written about J. W. Hulme and began carrying the bags in his men's clothing stores. That led to a *Wall Street Journal* article, which caught the attention of a new investor. To fashion publicists at top labels who tried to woo him to get coverage, Williams seemed inscrutable. He ignored their gifts and event invitations and wrote about only what interested him. And what interested him was businesses like J. W. Hulme—a highly specialized brand that made a single category of thing extremely well. There were many others: Tough Traveler backpacks of Schenectady, New York. Optimo Hats of Chicago. Schott NYC motorcycle jackets. Many of these companies had been around for decades, unaffected by fashion trends or economic cycles, quietly plugging away in near obscurity. Williams knew he'd found a good candidate for a feature when the company's website looked like a GeoCities page from 1995. Even better if there was no e-commerce portal. It signaled to him that all the value was in the product, not in the marketing.

For Williams, *ACL* was an extension of his marketing career— Red Wing and Buck Mason became his clients—but also a welcome break from the big personalities and high drama of the fashion world. When he contacted the factories of these small brands, many of them third- and fourth-generation family businesses, the owners welcomed him with open arms. "I would say, 'Tell me what you guys are doing. I just want to learn the history.' They'd be, like, 'Yeah, sure, come down to the factory.' It would be no bullshit, no publicist. And I'm coming from a world where you're just rude to everyone because it's fashion."

❦ ❦❦❦ ❦

One of Williams's favorite brands was the shoemaker Rancourt & Co. The state of American footwear manufacturing was even more dire than that of the clothing sector—only 1 percent of shoes were still made in America—and yet Rancourt, with roots half a century old, still produced its handmade, custom leather shoes and hand-sewn moccasins in Lewiston, Maine, once a shoemaking capital. Williams had bought several pairs of the brand's loafers and mocs over the years. As he told his *ACL* readers, he admired that Rancourt was both a brand and a factory, with workers and families for which it was responsible. The company was run by Mike Rancourt and his son, Kyle. Williams touted the Rancourts as knowing "a helluva lot about hand sewing and shoemaking in general. On top of that, they are good people who are doing their part to continue the shoecraft in Maine. Even if you take all of that away, Rancourt makes some damn fine shoes." Curious to see the process of shoemaking up close, I called Mike Rancourt and arranged to visit his factory.

Rancourt occupies half of a large, flat-roofed building surrounded by scrubland in a desolate neighborhood of Lewiston behind the city's hospital. When I arrived one November morning, Mike was in the front office area, tending to business matters. Fit and energetic for a guy in his upper sixties, with a big, square face partly obscured by a ball cap pulled low, Mike wore a fancy pair of shoes in faux alligator. "It's called a captain's oxford," he said of the style. "It goes way back to the sixties." He smiled. "I have a lot of shoes. A new product, I'll definitely wear it for at least a month to test it and see where the weaknesses are in the shoe, in the sole, wherever they may be. You might see me in the course of a year wear a dozen different pairs."

Mike explained that he had learned shoemaking from his father, Dave, a French Canadian who'd come to Maine in the 1940s and found work as a hand sewer in a factory in Freeport. In the mid-twentieth century, Maine, along with Massachusetts, was the center of shoemaking in the U.S., and practically every town, from Lewiston to Wilton to Dexter, had a shoe factory. Many of those New England shoe factories, along with the region's textile mills, were filled with French Canadians like Dave Rancourt. Around a million

French-speaking immigrants crossed the Canadian border in the mid-nineteenth and early twentieth centuries, and well into the '60s the common tongue in the mills and shoe factories along the Androscoggin River was French. With only a fifth-grade education, Dave rose to become a foreman and then superintendent at another factory. When the owner retired in 1967, he bought the business. Fifty years later, Mike could still remember sitting around the kitchen table with his father and his buddies the day Dave became a business owner. "They opened up a bottle of champagne. They gave me a little sip of it. They were all smiles," Mike said. "Everybody was cheering that my dad had just bought a factory. I was fourteen."

The other childhood memory of his father is a sensory one. "What sticks with me today," Mike said, "is the smells and odors of a shoe factory. You have leather and you have glue and you have threads and oils. That's really what struck me the most as a young person—the smells that my dad would bring home with him, on his clothes and hands, from work."

Dave's business specialized in hand sewing "uppers," the sections of the shoe that cover the foot above the sole, as well as hand sewing moccasins. After several years, he sold the upper-making factory to Quoddy, and in 1982, he approached Mike with the idea of starting their own company. Mike was twenty-eight at the time and working in the restaurant business. He saw shoemaking as akin to cooking: "You're taking raw materials, and you're turning it into something people love."

The timing couldn't have been worse—the year before, the Reagan administration had lifted shoe import quotas, and cheap footwear, mainly from Taiwan, was flooding the U.S. market. But in the stubborn, gutsy way of the kinds of apparel manufacturers that caught Williams's attention, Mike saw opportunity. With companies slashing costs and closing factories to stay competitive, there was a space in the market for higher-end footwear, which was labor-intensive. Mike and his father set up a factory in the old Lewiston Bleachery and Dye Works building downtown and started making handsewn shoes for Cole Haan, a brand that put a premium on the beauty of a shoe, the assembly and finish of the leathers. Mike took the approach to heart: "Make sure you're always on the premium side. Never dip your toe in the mass-produced, volume business."

After Dave retired in 1991, Mike and his wife, Debbie, started another manufacturing company, Maine Shoe. Their biggest customer was the Wisconsin-based dress-shoe brand Allen Edmonds, which hired Mike to make handsewn footwear, by then a dying craft hardly practiced anymore outside New England. In 1998, Mike and Debbie sold the business to Allen Edmonds, and Mike stayed on as president in charge of manufacturing in Lewiston. He later became vice president of sourcing and product development for the whole organization. For nearly a decade, the arrangement worked just fine, giving the Rancourts financial security while preserving the local tradition of shoemaking. But a private-equity firm bought Allen Edmonds in 2006, and during the forthcoming recession, the new owners decided to close the Maine operation completely and move a majority of its production to the Dominican Republic. Mike learned of the plan at a board meeting. He didn't react on the spot. He tried to understand the company's position even as he was absorbing the blow. "It was like a dagger in me," he said, "because it was my community."

Mike declined a new role within the company. Instead, he made the CEO an offer. He asked to buy the factory—*his* factory—back.

Just as his father had done, Mike invited his own son, Kyle, to join him in the business. Kyle had been preparing to go to graduate school in film, imagining a career for himself teaching film studies. But he saw his father's passion and excitement, and he respected what his grandfather had built. Together, Mike and Kyle reimagined the family business. Even as Rancourt remained a private-label manufacturer for other brands—Timberland, Sperry, Red Wing, Ralph Lauren (making shoes for the Olympic athletes)—Mike and Kyle began to design and make their own line of custom leather shoes. These they sold online, direct from the factory, to save on distribution costs. They were the shoes that Michael Williams got so excited about.

Out in the parking lot, Mike's truck bore the license plate SHOE 2, and as he led me out to the factory floor, he had the contented air of someone who does what he loves every day. "Still, when I open the factory door from the office, it strikes me," he said of the smells of leather and oils and glue.

Most of the employees were in their fifties or sixties, working-class rural white folks who'd spent their lives laboring in Maine's shoe factories, at G. H. Bass in Wilton or Livermore Falls Shoe in Livermore Falls or at L. L. Bean, which still manufactured its famous Bean boots in Brunswick. Some had come to work for Mike and his dad back in the 1980s and stayed through all the changes. But refugees from Angola and Congo had settled in the Lewiston area in recent years, and about a dozen of the new arrivals now worked for Rancourt, bringing new energy to the aging factory.

Mamie Kabulo had been orphaned in Congo at sixteen and later fled amid the country's political upheaval, eventually joining a sister in Maine. She'd been a seamstress in Congo and got a job in Rancourt's sewing department, running a pneumatic sewing machine and stitching uppers. The vibrantly colorful traditional African dresses Mamie wore made her stand out on the factory floor. "This is the first place where I've stitched leather," she said. "The material is different and challenging. Clothes are easy! But for shoes, you have to be focused."

As he walked among the machinery and workers, Mike said he tried to source as many components as he could in America. The leather hides, for example, came from the Horween tannery in Chicago. At Horween, Mike dealt with a guy about his age named Skip. His dad had dealt with Skip's dad. The thread was from a Lewiston company, Maine Thread, while the heels were made in Brockton, Massachusetts, by Montello Heel. Producing one pair of shoes took about 130 separate steps. Rancourt made penny loafers, boat shoes, wingtip brogues, dress boots, chukkas, and even a sneaker that Kyle had designed. But the brand was most famous for handsewn mocs.

Experienced hand sewers earned twenty dollars an hour at Rancourt. The job hadn't changed at all from the days when Mike's father started doing it, and the trade had typically been passed down from older to younger workers, but the transmission didn't always take. "We've attempted to train a dozen or so people in the last ten years," Mike said, taking me over to the department, "and none of them have succeeded at it." Another upstart shoemaker in Lewiston relied on an eighty-seven-year-old hand sewer. Indeed, Rancourt's five hand sewers were some of the last Americans doing it full-time.

For the next hour, I perched in that corner of the factory, watching the practitioners of a nearly lost craft.

A hand sewer stands at a workbench. Laid out on the bench are the tools of the trade: a knife, an awl, thread, tacks, lasting pliers (a curious tool with the jaws of pliers and the head of a hammer), needles, wax, and a small, rounded piece of wood that is used for rubbing out marks and nicks in the leather. The needles are thicker and longer than standard sewing needles and have rounded tips. A good hand sewer can produce about twenty pairs of shoes a day, depending on the style.

That November day, two sewers were off deer hunting, and another was out sick, leaving Jewel Rowe, the only woman in the department, and Jeff Rodrigue. Jewel's gray hair was pulled up, and she wore a blue work apron. She was friendly but terse, saying only that she'd been sewing for a long time and was, at sixty, two years from the age at which she'd told her husband she would retire.

Jeff looked about fifty, with light brown hair, a neatly kept beard, and glasses. He wore a black shirt decorated with car-racing patches. He had a Yankee reserve as well but soon warmed up. It was the Monday after the race for president had been called. "Had a good weekend," Jeff said, smiling. "The idiot Trump lost and I got a nice doe on Friday and took it to the butcher."

Early in his career, Jeff had worked for L. L. Bean, though his time with the Rancourts dated far enough back that he remembered Mike's dad. The shoe trade ran in Jeff's family. His father had been a hand sewer, too.

He'd just returned from his lunch break, and I watched him prepare for getting back to work. He wound white athletic tape around his fingers, much like a pro football linebacker gearing up for a game. The tape helped reduce calluses and guarded against slicing a finger when he yanked the waxed nylon thread tight.

Jeff was working on an order of bison-leather slippers. The process of making these shoes, derived from Native American methods that had been used for hundreds of years, involved only human hands, simple tools, and consummate skill. To "set up" the slipper for sewing, Jeff grabbed a precut piece of leather and pulled it over a plastic shoe form, known as a last, using the lasting pliers. This would be the shoe bottom. He then hammered tacks into the leather to hold it in place. He repeated this action with the top piece of leather, pulling and tacking so that the two pieces, top and bottom, were properly aligned on the last. If he didn't get them lined up right, the shoe would come out crooked when it was sewn. There was no guide—it was all done by eye and feel, as every leather reacts differently to the environment.

Next, Jeff secured the last in a bench vise to steady it for sewing. Holding two threaded needles, one in each hand, and the awl as well, he carefully pierced a hole into the leather with the awl. Then he stuck the needles through the hole, going in opposite directions, and pulled the thread tight in a flourish to make a stitch. He raised his arms out and away from his body after each stitch. His hands and arms moved quickly, fluidly, confidently, even though the job is physically taxing and one mistake can ruin the expensive leather. It was like watching a kind of ballet.

Jeff repeated the motion all the way around the shoe. The wooden rub stick had a grooved edge on one end, a channel cut into it that helped close the shoe. Jeff rubbed a little wax on the edges of the leather and ran the stick quickly around the seam, pushing the joined pieces of leather together until the two parts were seamlessly one.

"Takes a good one year to learn to do it," Jeff said, yanking the last stitch tight and loosening the shoe from the vise, ready to begin its mate.

He'd been doing it now for thirty years.

●━━●

In a letter to his readers that he titled "Heritage Land," Michael Williams once explained why he sought out and supported businesses like Rancourt & Co. and, in effect, workers like Jeff. "Why would I buy leather shoes from some random DTC company," he wrote, meaning an upstart direct-to-consumer online retailer, "when I could buy from Crockett & Jones or Red Wing, which have both been around for over 100 years and are still owned by families? Part of the reason I have focused so much of my attention on these types of businesses over the years is because I want them to continue to exist."

Chapter 6

The Sock Queen of Alabama

The name Gina Locklear decided on for her brand—Zkano—was intended to pay homage to the rich Cherokee history in DeKalb County. The name loosely translates as a state of "being good."

Zkano socks would be made with certified organic cotton, grown without pesticides. The yarn was colored with low-impact dyes that were free of heavy metals and used less water. Gina sourced the cotton from Texas and worked with a dyehouse in North Carolina, keeping the supply chain onshore. She wanted to set her socks apart and appeal to a younger generation who, like her, cared about their health and the environment. She would honor the sockmaking tradition of Fort Payne but do things in a new way.

Gina had already adopted an organic diet, and she knew that in northeast Alabama, where organic food wasn't widely available, organic clothing was a totally foreign concept. *Are your socks free-range?* She heard that one a lot from folks in town. Terry and Regina didn't get the whole organic thing, either. In fact, they needed convincing in general about Gina's business plan. The Locklears had always manufactured socks for other companies as contract knitters—they had no experience designing, marketing, and selling their own brand. Most of all, they didn't want their daughter to do something that she'd soon tire of or come to regret. "I know what it's like to run a factory," Terry warned her. He kept pushing Gina away. And Gina, willful and stormy as ever, kept pushing back.

In 2009, Emi-G Knitting effectively became two businesses. Terry and Regina continued to knit, seam, and board socks for various customers, everything from hospital socks to compression socks for horses. They sent the goods out to another mill in town for packaging and fulfillment. Production orders, or POs, came in fits and bursts now—nothing like the glory days with Russell Athletic, but business had recovered since the depths of 2008. Meanwhile, Gina focused on Zkano, selling her socks direct to consumers through a website, much as American Giant would.

Gina split her week between Birmingham and Fort Payne. On Sunday nights, she packed her travel bag with toiletries and a few days' worth of clothes, and first thing Monday morning, she got in her white Chevy Tahoe and drove to Fort Payne. It was an hour-and-a-half drive north, all interstate, and Gina had her personal landmarks along the route. When she saw the Trussville exit, it meant that she was out of city traffic and could relax a bit, start enjoying her morning coffee. After the little town of Steele, the landscape turned scenic and mountainous, and she knew she was halfway home. Noccalula Falls was the exit the family used to take to visit her grandparents on her mother's side, and often when she passed it, she thought of them.

She spent Mondays, Tuesdays, and Wednesdays at the mill, sleeping at her parents' house in her teenage bedroom. On Wednesdays after work, she drove back to Birmingham, where she tended to business matters the rest of the week. During busy production times, she spent Thursdays at the mill as well. Instead of tiring of the routine, the opposite happened. All her energy and passion seemed to have found the single-minded purpose they'd been seeking.

At first, Zkano's production runs were so small—forty or fifty pairs at a time, in only a few styles—that a single knitting machine in the mill could produce the entire line. But as her business grew, Gina took over a row of Anges. In 2012, she married Al Vreeland, the Birmingham labor attorney who'd been so impressed by Fort Payne's entrepreneurial spirit and its devotion to socks. They'd been introduced by mutual friends at a Birmingham restaurant, and as they waited for their table, Al had impressed Gina by talking about fixers and loopers. It hadn't taken him long to discover that she was consumed by making socks. "First thing she does when she wakes up in the morning, she doesn't brush her teeth," Al told me. "She pulls out her phone to see how many orders came in overnight. It's the first thing she wants to know."

Their wedding was in November, during the busy holiday production run. They had a small ceremony at the Loretto Chapel in Santa Fe, New Mexico, on a Saturday. "We came home on Sunday," Gina said. "And then I went to Fort Payne on Monday. That's my life."

Gina started a second line, Little River Sock Mill, doubling her workload. Zkano was a youthful riot of stripes and colors; Little River featured more sophisticated patterns, like florals, and was sold through a wholesale model at boutiques like Margaret O'Leary. Then Gina started making socks for Natalie Chanin of Alabama Chanin—her organic cotton, Natalie's designs. Customers sent her letters and emails praising the quality and originality of her socks, and whenever she set up at a farmers market, her booth was swarmed. Her socks were catching on.

So much so that *Martha Stewart Living* recognized Gina with an American Made award in 2015, which the magazine presented each year to ten makers around the country to encourage and support U.S. manufacturing. "The company caught our eye because, first, we love the socks, but also, it's such a good story," Martha Stewart told me. "Gina is rebuilding a business her parents built and making a town come to life again. It's a sensible business. Everyone needs socks." The award brought Gina national media attention, including a feature in *Martha Stewart Living*, which is how I came to learn about Zkano and the tradition of sockmaking in Fort Payne and found myself, a few months later, driving down Airport Road.

⚬ ⚬⚬⚬⚬ ⚬

The Locklears' mill is painted a soft gray, and the flower beds in front give it a more attractive appearance than its industrial neighbors. When I arrived, Gina was in the larger of the two buildings, where the offices were located, working on spring orders at her computer. She had long brown hair, warm eyes, and a straightforward manner. Dressed in dark jeans and a blue-and-white-checkered flannel shirt, she stood and shook my hand and said brightly, "Welcome to Fort Payne!"

Looking around Gina's office, I noticed that the decor was entirely related to hosiery. In the corner, a shelf was heaped with cones of yarn in bright colors. The main wall was taken up by two corkboards, each with socks pinned to it. These were SKUs, or sample styles, from the line currently in production, Gina said. The unusual-looking rug we stood on was made of factory seconds—socks rejected because of runs or other flaws.

At age thirty-six, Gina had been making socks for seven years by that point. "We're in a place of happy right now," she said, explaining that sales were good and more stores were picking up her lines. She was still basking in the glow of the award, which had included a trip to New York to attend a banquet for the honorees. Also, the humble sock was having a high-fashion moment. Socks paired with dresses were showing up in the pages of *Vogue*, and models had walked a Miu Miu show in marled and argyle socks.

"Let me show you some of our socks," Gina said, going over to a table piled with samples. Picking one up, she said, "This is our signature style. It's a textured herringbone." Grabbing another, a cushioned short sock, or "no-show," she said, "You have people who want a cushion sock, and you have people for whom they're too thick. I personally love a cushion sock. It is so, so soft. I wear these to the gym." In the fall and winter, Gina wore over-the-knee socks matched with long dresses during the daytime and wool socks to bed at night. In the summers, she wore no-shows with sneakers. I couldn't see what socks she had on that day under her brown boots. (I was wearing gray socks my mother had given me for Christmas.)

For all her success, Gina had just two part-time employees at that point, and she handled practically every aspect of the business herself. She chose the season's colors, came up with the designs, ordered the yarn, did Zkano's social media and marketing, and processed credit card orders. She even acted as the customer service department, personally answering every call, email, Facebook message, and letter of praise or complaint. In the early days, before she brought in the part-timer to inspect and package socks, she did that job, too, while sitting on the living room floor in her parents' house at night and watching TV. The workload reflected not a reluctance to cede control but sheer economic necessity. Gina relied on her parents' business to support her brand, and as long as that was the case, she could not increase her overhead. As Gina explained all this, my eyes fell on a Zkano advertisement framed and hanging near the office door: a pair of shapely legs sporting calf-height socks. Gina laughed. She was also a sock model. The legs were hers.

Gina's office shared a wall with her father's; Regina's was down the hall. That afternoon, the two of them joined us for lunch at the Big Mill, which hadn't been a sock factory for decades and was now an antique store and café. I liked the Locklears immediately and felt a kinship with them, having grown up in a small town of faded industry myself. Our hometowns were linked, I realized, not only by the same Appalachian chain but also by a common culture that ran down through those mountains, eight hundred miles to their southern boundary. When Terry mentioned Alabama's origins in Fort Payne, I remembered how the band's song "Mountain Music" used to play all the time in my hometown.

Terry and Regina had been high school sweethearts—they'd wed in June 1965, following Regina's graduation—and they had the easy rapport of a long-married couple, with the deeper bond of having worked together for so many years. Terry was friendly and outgoing. At seventy-one, he bore a slight resemblance to Bill Clinton—same bulb nose and full white hair. Regina, who at seventy was quieter and more cautious in nature than her husband, had cropped dark hair and glasses. When the subject of their first mill, in the former chicken house, came up, Terry said bashfully, "I'm almost ashamed to tell you about it. Aw, I'll just tell you."

"Tell him about the birds—it's a funny story," Regina prompted.

"We had no air-conditioning in that building," Terry said. "It had doors on both ends. Big doors. Like the whole end would open up. We would open those doors to get a little air going through there, and birds would actually fly through while you were working."

That time starting out had bonded the family together, and the memories of it remained vivid. In the afternoons, after knitting all day, Regina would drive down the mountain to pick up the girls from school. Then it was back up to the mill, where Gina and Emily would pass the time until ten o'clock, when they all went home. Gina was on the cusp of her teens and just discovering boys. Stuck with her parents on a remote mountaintop every day, she passed the hours listening to a boom box and pining. "Today," she said, "if I hear 'Neon Moon' by Brooks and Dunn or 'Achy Breaky Heart' by Billy Ray Cyrus, it takes me right back to that time."

I asked them how Emi-G had survived when so many other mills hadn't made it. Why were the Locklears still in business? Terry said that he had often wondered that himself. He'd come up with a theory: "The only way we made it is 'cause we were lean and we didn't have any debt," he said. "We owed for nothing. We just didn't go away. We kept sittin' here thinking something would come along. Sure enough, it did."

Indeed, Gina's appearance in the mill had changed the course of the business and her parents' lives. They no longer thought about closing the mill and retiring. They felt reinvigorated. "I guess what Gina has done with this organic stuff is brought new life to what we do," said Terry. "To me, it's just almost like starting all over again."

Regina added, "She knows more about the makeup of a sock than I do. And she can run a machine. I can't run a machine. She's taught us so much. So much. A lot more than we ever taught her." Gina's commitment and drive astonished her parents every day. "She's *on fire*," Regina said.

That morning, Gina had shown me the heart of the mill: the room where socks were made. She led me down a hallway and opened a heavy, aluminum-clad soundproof door to the knitting room. It was about the size of a basketball court, windowless and fluorescently lit, with four rows of machines running lengthwise. The machines—Anges—were boxy, like kitchen ovens, and teal in color. Above each one, at a little higher than eye level, creels hung from the ceiling. These metal racks held spools of off-white yarn that was fed down into the knitting machines. You could tell immediately which machines were dedicated to Gina's socks, because the yarn hanging in the creels was red, blue, pink, orange, yellow, purple—every color of the rainbow. All that fantastic floating color gave Gina's side of the knitting room a busy, cheerful atmosphere.

In foreign factories, the cost of labor is so cheap that there is often a worker assigned to each machine. In U.S. plants, one worker may be responsible for an entire production line. At first, Emi-G seemed to contain no employees, only autonomously running machines. Far down one of the rows, I finally spotted a stocky man dressed in blue work clothes. He was bent over in concentration. Gina pointed out an orange light on a pole beside the machine. The light was blinking, signaling a malfunction. "That's Kenny," she said, speaking loudly to make herself heard over the high-pitched din of the factory. Kenny Young was a line knitter, overseeing all forty Anges on her parents' side. He worked alongside a "creeler," who was responsible for keeping the correct yarns on the creels during knitting.

Gina led me over to one of the Anges. It was knitting a new style of Zkano sock. Thin metal fingers atop the machine moved up and down rapidly, pulling in orange yarn. Inside, I saw the silvery flash of the needles—this Ange had 144 of them.

Down the left side of the machine ran a clear plastic tube. Its function was initially a puzzle to me. Then, with a sudden *whoosh* and *POP!*, a striped orange sock, complete but for the unseamed toe, spit out of the tube. Surprised and amazed, I burst out laughing. "I love that!" exclaimed Gina. She had seen that finish thousands of times, but she hadn't lost her own delight at it.

Before Gina came along, the mills in Fort Payne, including Emi-G, had always made essentially one type of sock: a white tube sock, the kind bought in packs of six at big-box stores. White tube socks had built Fort Payne the way milk chocolate bars had built Hershey, Pennsylvania. In large part that's because it's easy for a mill to crank them out. The creels are numbered so that the spools loaded onto them are fed into the machine in a certain order that corresponds to a pattern. For white tube socks, a worker loads spools of white cotton yarn, elastic, and nylon; sets the machines to knit a basic pattern; and lets them run and run. Back in the '90s, one of Bob Yoe's contract knitters for DeSoto Mills made a single style of basic sock continuously, six days a week, for four years straight.

But Gina envisioned fashion socks with pattern and color and whimsy, and to make them, you couldn't set the Anges and let them run ad infinitum. You had to program the complex designs with computer software and come up with new designs each season. (Basic socks were also designed with computer software, but the programs were much simpler than those required to produce a fashion sock.) It meant continuously changing the settings—the order in which the machines took in yarn—and using a richer palette of color beyond off-white. Gina required technical expertise to achieve what she wanted. For that, she relied on Vance Veal.

Vance was from the Fort Payne of old. His grandparents, his mother, his sister, and his three brothers had all worked in the mills. Vance's initiation came at sixteen, when he took an after-school job at Cooper Hosiery as a sock inspector. Later, that job became automated, but back in 1984, an inspector had to stick their arm up a knit sock and turn it inside out to check for runs in the yarn. During an eight-hour shift, Vance turned more than a thousand socks. The repeated friction wore the hair off his arms. Eventually it rubbed his skin raw until his forearms bled. He had to take a week off work to heal. But he was making $3.35 an hour, good money to a teenager in those days, and he loved the atmosphere. "The smell got me," Vance said. "The oils, the machines. It was a new experience, and I liked the camaraderie."

Wanting to get off third shift at another mill so that he could spend evenings with his wife and newborn son, Vance had come to work for the Locklears in 1994. He replaced Terry's old fixer, Sam, who'd spent his life working on Banners and couldn't grasp the automated Anges. Terry had to get rid of the blowtorch because it was the first thing Sam reached for when a part broke. Terry called Vance's arrival "a blessing," and over the years, Vance had assumed the role of Emi-G's production manager and plant manager. He was the only employee Terry and Regina had kept when they'd hit their lowest point and had to lay everyone else off.

Gina had known Vance since she was a teenager. When she spotted him working in another part of the knitting room and called him over, she introduced him to me by saying, "This is Vance—he's like family."

Gina and Vance proved to be a good team. He was easygoing and didn't have a problem taking orders from a woman, which was unusual in a factory environment. And though Vance wasn't a big talker—he had a way of nodding and mumbling, his lower lip bulging with the snuff he'd been dipping since age fourteen—he displayed a keen intelligence around any kind of machinery. Gina needed every bit of Vance's patience and skill because what she wanted to do was uncharted territory for them all. After making plain white socks all his life, Vance was suddenly on the phone with technicians from the Czech Republic, learning how he might code in the pattern so the machines would knit a four-color flower on a curvy stem. He took it as an intellectual challenge.

"A basic sock is easy. When you run a pattern, you got to watch every little detail about a sock," Vance told me. "You don't want a sock with the wrong color in a star or a flower."

"I remember when we made our first stripe together, Vance and me," Gina said. "I didn't think we could make a stripe. It was the simplest stripe ever, but I was about to do cartwheels in the mill because we could do something other than a basic sock. That was the beginning."

As Gina and Vance unlocked new capabilities, socks in candy colors and quirky designs began filling the knitting room. An orange polka-dot anklet on a sage base. A slouch in black-and-white stripes. Socks in six different yarn colors. Socks featuring tiny flying geese, jumping foxes, tumbling dice, and antique bicycles. One Christmas, Gina designed a deer head with a rack of antlers on a sock she named the Buck. Her favorite patterns were vintage florals: a winter jasmine with a delicate brown stem, a dandelion with puffy pink florets, a curvy-vined rose. Vance figured out how to run the complex programs on machines designed to make only very basic socks. As Terry put it, "Vance tricked the machines into doing what he wanted." Gina grew more confident in her designs, too. In time, the florals became as intricate as antique wallpaper patterns, rendered in yarn.

Gina was drawing on iconography of the South and of her own life to tell a story through her socks. One pattern she designed was inspired by traditional Southern quilts. Another featured a camellia, which was the state flower of Alabama and Gina's favorite. She and Al had planted them in their yard in Birmingham. A dog lover, she often put dogs on socks—retrievers, terriers. She gave every style a name, and the names had personal meanings, too. Lucy, a polka-dot creation, honored Gina's grandmother; Forrest, a men's ribbed crew, referenced a street in Fort Payne on which she'd once lived. One year, the Zkano line included a men's sock with tiny El Caminos on it. When I asked why that model of car, Gina said, "My dad used to have one and drove me around in it when I was a kid."

For especially complex patterns, Gina and Vance sometimes spent half the day tweaking a design and running dozens of samples to get one good SKU. In a honeyed voice, Gina said, "Vance is the most patient person ever."

Vance blushed at the compliment. "Gina keeps me on my toes," he told me. "She's made me better at what I do."

Later, with Vance out of earshot, Gina's voice got low and serious. "If something happened to Vance, I wouldn't know what we would do," she said. "He programs. He fixes the machines when they're not running right—which is a lot of the time. He runs my parents' side of the business dealing with the customers, so that's another role. He's truly the backbone of our socks."

Vance Veal belonged to a rare, vanishing breed in Fort Payne. "When the sock industry left," Gina said, "a lot of the workers left town. And their knowledge left, too."

It was indicative of a larger problem in textiles—a lack of qualified workers—that was in turn the result of being in an industry in long-term decline. Howard Cooley, the former executive at Jockey, had worked in the 1960s and '70s as an industry consultant, helping to open new factories. He went from town to town, factory to factory, spending anywhere from six to nine months setting up the production of trousers, jeans, shirts, and outerwear. Through all that time he spent in mills, Cooley told me, he came to understand the subtle, incremental way in which workers gained knowledge at a factory. "It's handed down," he said. "People go to work in their teens or twenties, and they work with older textile workers, and they learn. There's a lot of what I call generational knowledge." Workers also learned by doing. Running a loom or napper every day for years, they developed an intimate understanding of the machine; they got to know its capabilities and quirks as one knows a family member. Danny Swafford, the factory owner in Tennessee, cut the garments himself, and he was excellent at it. "In all the years I worked with him," said Taylor Johnston, the founder of Gamine, the women's workwear brand, "I could count on one hand the mess-ups. He did it all. And it was precise. You can find a factory in L.A. to make denim. You cannot find a Danny Swafford." When a mill closed or an industry left a town, all that accumulated expertise disappeared. For the past forty years, few new workers had been trained up. "That's one of the reasons you can't recreate textiles in America very well today," Cooley said. "Top management is easy; they just deal with the money. But middle management and foremen, okay? Lead operators that run textile mill equipment? It's very hands-on stuff."

In the onetime sock capital of the world, Gina would have much trouble finding another veteran programmer like Vance or a young fixer to train up.

One evening, Gina and I stopped for takeout at a barbecue place in town. It turned out that the guy behind the counter, a broad-shouldered, round-faced man in his early thirties named Bo Doeg, knew the Locklear family. Bo's family had been involved in socks, too.

"I grew up in the business," he said. "We had a machine shop, and it closed down. There's no market for it anymore."

It was entirely likely that Bo's family business had fabricated parts for Locklear Hosiery, the mill owned by Gina's uncle Roland, or Abel Hosiery, which was run by another uncle, her mother's brother. Roland and Terry's nephew, Gina's cousin David, also ran a mill. Bo didn't say how he knew the Locklears, and anyway, all those mills were gone now, like his family's machine shop.

While we waited for our food, Gina and I chatted with Bo about the hosiery industry. He had a lot to say on the subject.

"Everybody had a job," he told me. "That was a big thing throughout the town. This is a different world than it used to be."

"You remember that buzz that used to be here?" Gina said.

Bo nodded. "Hosiery Week." Painting a picture for me, he said, "Imagine Mardi Gras, but for socks. Every local business except for the restaurants shut down. There was a huge softball game that the whole town went to. There was a golf tournament. There were giveaways, banners hanging up across the roads, vendors all over town, bowling tournaments. Anything that you could really think of to bring together the people that made socks."

Fort Payne hadn't hosted Hosiery Week in many years. I asked Bo and Gina why the town couldn't continue to celebrate the event. After all, there were a dozen or so sock mills still in operation, from major outfits like Cooper and Renfro to smaller mills like Emi-G.

Bo shook his head. "How do you celebrate something when you walk into a mill that's been there for a hundred and eight years and the owner says, 'I'm sorry. I know your whole family has worked for my family, but this is the last check I'm going to give you'?"

Bo's playful tone disappeared. "Let me put it to you this way," he went on. "Have you driven through Fort Payne? Have you seen the vast number of empty buildings? Can you imagine the number of bodies it took to fill those mill buildings with workers? Now imagine none of them getting a paycheck, and the nearest job is forty miles in the direction that you've never been. Growing up, I never knew anyone's parents where they'd say, 'I just can't get a job.' It wasn't that way. Back then, even a shitty-paying sock mill job was a guaranteed three hundred plus a week. That's where you're really busting your hump all day. But if you were good and consistent, you could get a production job. And I knew guys making seven hundred, eight hundred a week boarding socks or finishing socks or working in dyehouses. If you had the desire, you could've gone and gotten a job. Now, if you have the desire, you got to take minimum wage to outbid the teenagers."

I had driven through town and seen the empty buildings. Along Gault Avenue, Fort Payne's main street, half the storefronts were vacant. The downtown was drained of vitality. The commerce and bustle now out by the interstate exit, with its chain restaurants and hotels. Earlier that afternoon, I'd visited the Fort Payne Hosiery Museum, which had taken over one of the old storefronts downtown. It was there that I saw a fabled Banner knitting machine up close and was shown the original steam whistle from the Big Mill. The whole experience made me sad. Fort Payne was rightfully proud of its history, but the exhibits spoke volumes about the places in America that used to make things. Instead of a thriving industry that brought prosperity to a community, now there was only a museum for it.

Industry creates a texture to communities that goes beyond the strict number of people it employs. The sock mills had been active in the local community, holding blood drives and sponsoring the Boy Scouts and Little League. At one Prewett plant, the employees had established a Helping Hands fund. If someone had a medical bill or their house burned down or their child had a special need and they didn't have the money, the fund took care of it. It was financed by the workers themselves, who dropped a dollar or two into a box each pay period. As the millworkers searched for new jobs and built new lives, they scattered, and that closeness was lost.

Some relocated to Honduras with Gildan. Some found jobs driving forklifts at the Children's Place distribution center or working for another company in town. A few of the managers took roles with Westinghouse Electric in Birmingham. Rhonda Whitmire, one of Emi-G's employees, had worked for Prewett Mills her whole adult life, almost thirty years, rising to become supervisor of quality control at Prewett's Cherokee finishing plant (where she'd run the Helping Hands fund). After Gildan closed the plant, Rhonda enrolled at the local community college to study nursing, but she didn't like it. She quit the program and took a job with Plasman, a local company that manufactured plastic parts for cars. "We sanded parts with palm sanders. It was just one of those fill-in jobs that you hate to talk about," Rhonda told me, explaining that her brother-in-law saved her when he mentioned that Terry and Regina Locklear were hiring.

Even after more than a decade, Rhonda remembered vividly the summer day when she and her coworkers stood in the Cherokee parking lot, crying and hugging one another and exchanging addresses and phone numbers, trying to stay connected. "It makes you feel shocked and numb and hurt all at the same time," she said. "It was just a heartbreaking thing. It was like a death, actually, the last day."

When the mills left, the thing that had bound the community together, the work that had given the people of Fort Payne a common purpose and identity for an entire century—that was gone.

Our food came out, and Bo rang us up.

"I love socks, and I grew up in it, and there's a special place in it for me," he said. "But there's a lot of animosity towards the sock world now."

He handed Gina and me our barbecue dinners, finished with the subject. "Let's get some grub on."

● ◄◄► ◄

I was impressed by Gina's tireless drive and iron will. For all the challenges she faced, for all the economic devastation around her, she would not be deterred.

But the more time I spent with her, the more I also noticed cracks in that cheery, determined front. The business remained touch and go. The orders for her parents' side slowed again, and Emi-G had to lay off fifteen people and reduce to one shift. Gina's organic lines alone could not support the mill. The future still felt precarious.

Sometimes, a tone of worry and even fear would creep into Gina's voice when she was talking about the future of her business. Her parents were getting older—what would happen if they had health problems and decided to retire, or when they died? Some years back, Vance had been diagnosed with Parkinson's disease; he'd had three surgeries to slow the symptoms, including having wires implanted in his brain to stop his tremors, but it was a degenerative disease, and it was starting to slow him some at work. When Gina spoke of Vance's condition and the possibility of losing him, her voice thickened with emotion. "He's truly the backbone of our socks," she repeated to me. "I don't know what I'd do without Vance."

She was also worried about her own future. Her sister already had a family over in Cullman, and Gina had thought about having children, too—but with her crazy schedule, how? Her weekly commute from Birmingham was exhausting and, in the long term, unsustainable. There was always some crisis at the mill to deal with, and living ninety minutes away complicated that. The Anges were like misbehaving kids, forever acting up. That pointed to another problem: Anges were fast becoming outdated, like the Banners before them, and sourcing parts was getting harder and harder.

These worries hovered in the background of Gina's life like time bombs, and she went cold with fear if she thought about them for too long. Tough and determined as she was, her business was fragile.

"I'll just be honest, it's been a struggle," she said.

It was only when she was making socks that her stress and worries dissipated. When Gina Locklear was engaged in the craft she loved, a calm, single-minded focus came over her.

One afternoon, I watched Gina working on a new design—another beloved camellia flower. She was in the office kitchen looking over samples, or "swatches," piled on a folding table. She was joined by Rhonda Whitmire. Now in her early fifties, Rhonda packaged online orders and inspected socks as Emi-G's quality-control manager. Unofficially, she was Gina's in-house design consultant. An excellent colorist, Rhonda created color palettes for Zkano designs, and spent more and more of her time in a product development role.

"We're small around here," Gina said, "and we all wear a lot of hats."

Gina held up a sample of the camellia sock. It was just a stub of fabric. To save yarn, a sample sock was knit only a few inches long, just enough to see the design being considered. Each flower had clusters of rose-colored petals, and the edge of each petal was outlined in brown yarn. Curling vines made of blue yarn and leaves in a darker blue were knit on a green base. "We love viny things," Gina said. "And I also felt the pattern had a romantic, antique quality about it, and I really loved that."

Still, something was off to her eye.

"Call me crazy," Gina said to Rhonda. "What do you think about switching it? Making the vine color the leaf. And then doing Denim for the vine."

"Denim vine, Navy leaf?" said Rhonda, using shorthand Pantone names.

"Might get it better, might not," Gina said. Rhonda headed back to the knitting room to have another sample made.

The camellia would be sold in three colorways. Gina had to figure out combinations that would look good together yet be distinct and appealing to customers. Between the heel, toe, and base colors, plus the various colors within the design, there were almost infinite possibilities. "It's amazing how something so small, a couple of knitted rows in a sock, can throw the whole thing off," Gina said. "And also, you have to consider, I'm not a designer. I don't know the technical approach, so I stumble a lot. My husband got me a book about color theory. But I think feeling my way is better." Gina noticed socks everywhere she went and was constantly making notes for future designs. She loved playing with color, pattern, texture. "I can get inspired by a car sitting in front of a building and how the colors go together." One early color-blocked sock was inspired by a Diane von Furstenberg dress.

Rhonda returned with a new version.

"I like the vine part," Rhonda said, showing Gina the sample. "Now it's the leaf. I'm just wondering what Eggplant would do."

Gina studied the new sample, hesitating, still unsatisfied. Then she homed in on a tiny detail: each leaf had a dark line down the middle—just one or two knitted rows—to mimic the midrib of a real leaf. Gina said, "If we change the center of the leaf, could that work?"

Rhonda nodded. "I see exactly what you're talking about."

Rhonda marched back out to the knitting room, and this time I followed. She turned down a row and stopped at the machine where Vance stood waiting. Opposite them was the sample cart, which functioned much like a painter's palette, piled with spools of yarn in fantastic shades: Purple Orchid. Misty Rose. Orange Pop. Gulf Coast. French Roast. Coral. Cornflower. Eggplant. Clearwater. Aqua. Asphalt. Rhonda handed Vance the unsatisfactory sample and pointed out the change that Gina wanted.

Reaching up, Vance found the spool on the creel that corresponded to the central vein of the leaf in the pattern that he'd coded. He swapped out the yarn. He pressed a button. The fingers bobbed, the needles hammered. When the new sample popped out of the vacuum tube a minute later, Rhonda grabbed it and walked back to the kitchen.

"Let's see," Gina said, holding all three versions in her hands.

Her face lit up in pleasure. "Oh my Lord, that's *beautiful*. This is my favorite sock, let me just go ahead and tell you. I wish they all turned out this way. Because I am absolutely in love with those colors. In love. In love."

"It's gonna be a major seller," Rhonda said.

* —◆— ◀

Gina kept growing her business, and around 2018, she passed a milestone. Her brand could now support itself without the help of her parents' private-label orders. It wasn't like she saw numbers on a spreadsheet and bells went off. It was more of a feeling. Orders for her socks were rolling in steadily, and she was confident they would continue.

One day, a truck drove down Airport Road and delivered five brand-new knitting machines. The Italian-made Lonati machines, which cost $40,000 each, were next-generation technology—Lonatis had greater pattern capability than Anges and could knit socks and close the toes all in one process, eliminating that extra, labor-intensive step. It meant that Maria Pascual, a millworker who had moved between the Emi-G and Zkano sides, jumping in wherever she was needed, could stop spending so much time seaming and help Gina full-time in fulfillment.

While her parents continued to use Anges to make basic white socks, Gina put the Lonatis on her line. The company sent a technician from Italy to show Vance how they worked. Two years later, the mill ordered five more. It'd taken nearly a decade, but Gina's brands—"my babies," she called them—were sturdy enough to stand on their own.

Chapter 7

American Flannel

In late 2017, James McKinnon received a call from Bayard Winthrop, asking for his help and advice on the flannel project. James knew Bayard a little; he'd met him a few times and once heard him give a fiery speech at an industry conference about reviving American manufacturing. The speech had impressed James, because showing grand ambition was uncommon among textile and apparel people. Like beaten dogs, domestic manufacturers kept their heads down, simply hoping to survive another day.

At fifty, James was a year older than Bayard. Like him, he came from an upscale suburb within commuting distance of New York City (in his case, Scarsdale). James had also distinguished himself in the beleaguered industry as a beacon of possibility and a risk-taker. "He's a guy that's willing to figure out how to dance between the raindrops," Phil Goetz, a former business partner, said of him. But where Bayard was a start-up founder, James managed a multigenerational textile company, with six divisions and an office in a highrise building in Midtown Manhattan. When Bayard was building his first supply chains, James was already a delegate to the National

Cotton Council, a schmoozer who knew every major player left in the game.

In the mid-1950s, James's paternal grandfather, Malcolm Mc-Kinnon, was one of the founders of Cotswold Industries, a textile "converter." A converter purchased fabric from various mills and had it sent to finishing plants to be produced to spec for customers, overseeing the process as a kind of middleman. For years, Cotswold had supplied the headliners and seat covers for Ford. It sold inner-lining cloth to the Endicott-Johnson Shoe Company, which in the mid-twentieth century produced fifty million pairs of shoes a year. Made-in-America textiles went into other made-in-America goods. Malcolm's two sons, Floyd (known as Wink) and Jim, joined the family firm, and in the 1970s and '80s, they moved into the lucra-tive business of pocketing, supplying denim makers like Wrangler and Levi's with pocket lining.

Wink McKinnon's oldest son seemed positioned to strike out for success in a different direction: the new digital economy. In the early 1990s, James and a friend cofounded an executive recruiting firm that specialized in placing talent with Mozilla and other fledg-ling internet companies. But, as with Bayard, it was manufacturing actual products that called to him. When a partner died suddenly, the opportunity arose for James to join Cotswold. He jumped at it. "Working with my father and working for the family business, I felt I couldn't pass up," he reflected. "There are certain connections you have with a parent, hopefully. That was ours."

James joined Cotswold in 1994, the year NAFTA became law. The trade treaty was sold by lawmakers on both sides as a win for the American people—a symbolic embrace of global free trade that would lead to hundreds of thousands of onshore jobs and lower prices for consumers. The detractors were few and far between. While running for president two years earlier, Ross Perot was ridiculed when he forewarned of "the great sucking sound" Americans would hear when U.S. companies relocated across the Mexican border. Perot proved to be right, and the textile and apparel industry, true to its nature and history, led the charge in seeking cheaper labor.

James "followed the needle," as textile people say. His first few years in the business, he traveled to Mexico and other Latin American countries, establishing contacts with local manufacturers. "The pocketing business was in a mad rush to get there," he said. "It was the Wild West of opportunity."

By the end of the decade, Big Apparel was on the move again, to even lower-cost countries: Bangladesh, Vietnam, India, Sri Lanka, and especially China. It didn't take a PhD in economics to understand that if Levi's 501s or Gap chinos were made in overseas factories, the pocket lining would be, too. James racked up frequent-flier miles trying to secure relationships with factory owners in those markets so that Cotswold wouldn't lose its biggest clients.

He made his first trip to China in 1997. He was met at the crumbling old Shanghai airport by a Western facilitator, a German named Reinhardt, and taken to a denim mill in the city. "We arrived at this place, and I literally told him, 'I don't think I can go in that building because I might die,'" James recalled. "It was held up with bamboo sticks. The floor was dirt. The Chinese, at that time, chain-smoked. I'm in this factory. I was absolutely frightened out of my mind that the place would either collapse or go up in a blazing fire at any moment. I was tugging at Reinhardt's coat—'I think we've seen enough.

Let's get out of here.' The worst part was they were pouring the indigo chemicals into the river."

Less than two years later, however, Cotswold was operating a sales office in Hong Kong and manufacturing in mainland China. Pocketing was a basic commodity product, meaning that no company had an advantage over another in making it. Cotswold was competing purely on price. The surest way to keep the family business going for another generation was to follow the herd and outsource production. "You were either doing that," James said, "or going down."

Still, the McKinnons remained committed to American manufacturing. Cotswold owned a weaving mill in South Carolina, Central Textiles. The McKinnons discovered that you could manufacture in the U.S. profitably if you made technical and specialty fabrics. They diversified into any niche market that might generate sales, making the unseen materials that underpinned daily life—the stretchy fabric that goes into Band-Aids, the bias fabric that wraps around the copper cores of telephone cables, the cloth in military ammunition bandoliers, the lining for movie screens. Cotswold supplied blue oxford fabrics for Catholic school uniforms, flame-resistant toques to culinary workers, and cloth filter bags to gold and silver miners. The company made dress shirts under its own brand, Wingfield, which were sold online. It made fabric wall coverings for Marriott hotel rooms and booties for hospital staff.

It was James who dreamed up many of these obscure revenue streams. "I did not have any experience in the finance side, nor the manufacturing nor the science side. I told my dad very early on that the only way I would be of use was to go and find markets and try to create rain."

James's reputation as a rainmaker had led Bayard to seek him out. Not long after, when James had other business in San Francisco, they arranged to meet at the American Giant offices. There, Bayard repeated to James what he'd been told about flannel—that making it stateside again might be impossible. Unlike everyone else Bayard had asked, James responded, "It can be done. You just need the will to do it."

In truth, James was bluffing a little; he hadn't seriously looked into the process. But he found himself excited by the possibility. "You start to put the pieces together in your head. You think, *Can we actually do this?*"

When he got back to New York, James gathered his employees together in a room and asked their opinion. Not one of them thought it was still possible to manufacture flannel domestically. James stood up and wrote on a whiteboard all the necessary steps, like he was diagramming a football play: YARN SPINNING > YARN DYEING > WARPING > WEAVING > NAPPING/FINISHING > SEWING THE SHIRTS.

"I said, 'Guys, take a look. This can be done here. This can be done here.'" He ticked down the list. "'This can be done here and here.' Until finally the team looked at me and said, 'Huh.'"

＊ ⬤⬤⬤ ＊

James and Cotswold agreed to "quarterback" the flannel project. In practical terms, this meant that James would find the U.S. factories to produce the flannel fabric and that he would oversee the manufacturing journey for Bayard and his team back in San Francisco. Through the winter and spring of 2018, the two men were in daily phone contact, laying the groundwork for the project.

Everything—the dyeing, the weaving of the fabric—flowed from the design of the shirt. But the design of the shirt had to take into account the strictures of the rest of the process. Back in San Francisco at American Giant's office, the label's design director, Sharon Aris, began to consider the creative possibilities and, of equal concern to her, the limitations. Like James's, Sharon's career had closely tracked the apparel industry's mass migration offshore. A native of England, she had a degree in fashion design from Kingston University, in southwest London. Her first job, in the late '80s, was designing for the French denim brand Girbaud, which made its jeans in European mills and factories. In the '90s, she moved to America and worked for the California sportswear company Esprit. At Esprit, practically "every single thing was made offshore, in Asia," Sharon told me. As a designer, she came up with concepts, designs, and colors at the brand's San Francisco office, then sent "tech packs" (the set of directions or blueprints for constructing a garment) to Esprit's office in Hong Kong. Every six months, Sharon traveled to Hong Kong to do fittings with models on-site and finalize the designs. The clothes were produced in mainland China, Eastern Europe, and India.

As time went on, at Esprit and other brands Sharon worked for, design became more and more disconnected from production. She would email tech packs to factories in Asia or Eastern Europe, get samples back three months later, and never meet anyone involved in making the clothes. Working from a distance of five thousand miles, it was impossible to see the clothes in progress and make beneficial tweaks. There was rarely any collaboration between the designer and the head of sewing at the factory. The system was almost entirely cost-driven. "You get it at a price that makes everyone happy but the designers," said Sharon. Her last design job before American Giant was at a children's clothing company that manufactured overseas and utilized a product design management system. "It's basically data entry," Sharon said. "You add a code, like P-1604—that's a certain button in black. You literally go in and plug these codes into the system from a catalog of coded components." Sharon liked the company and its culture, but after working there for two and a half years, "I felt so detached," she said. "I really was ready to get my hands back on product. See it on the body, fit it, touch it."

Designing for American Giant proved to be unlike any job Sharon had had in three decades in fashion. A button vendor would visit the label's office, open up a case, and present their wares to her. Face-to-face, Sharon and the manufacturer could collaborate. "You say, 'Instead of shiny, can you make it matte?' They're, like, 'Yeah, yeah, we can make it matte. We'll put it through a tumbler.'" In 2016, Bayard decided to add denim to the line. Sharon traveled to Georgia to visit Mount Vernon Mills, the 170-year-old cotton mill that had been hired to weave the denim. She looked through racks of sample fabrics with the millworkers. She spent six months working with the factory to get the fabric right. Was it strong? Did it have enough stretch? How did it wash? After she settled on the fabric blend, she had the guys at the office back in San Francisco wear-test the jeans for three months. "From fabrics to trim to sewing, it's all at a human level," Sharon said. "Which you don't get working offshore. There's no way you could."

The trade-off for this level of hands-on control was having to source all materials in the United States. It was like being the chef at a locavore restaurant located in the desert. Fabrics like merino wool, oxford cloth, and canvas were scarcely available domestically. Textile innovation now took place in Asia and Europe, which meant that many technical fabrics, like those found in performance outerwear, were impossible to get. At one point, Bayard had looked into adding corduroy to the line, until he discovered that while the weaving, shearing, and finishing could still be done in the U.S., the cutting of the wales could not. No factory had the machines anymore.

Every designer, even very famous ones like Stella McCartney and Tom Ford, faces some technical limitations. But limitations—and finding constructive ways around them—defined Sharon's job. Many secondary suppliers had moved offshore or gone out of business, leaving just a handful of vendors for zippers, buttons, clasps, and other trimmings. Another example: Sharon loved Riri zippers—their beautiful metal finishes could change the visual language of a garment—but Riri was a Swiss company, off-limits. Instead, American Giant used zippers by YKK, a Japanese firm with a factory in Georgia. Not all American-made labels were as strict. Buck Mason, the direct-to-consumer sportswear brand that was an American Giant competitor, cut and sewed its jeans in Los Angeles, but the denim was Japanese, while the hardware was from China and the dyes from India. Todd Snyder tried to balance his Asian production with Made in the U.S.A., finding "little pockets" of capability that remained, like sweaters, denim and suits. Natalie Chanin of Alabama Chanin used domestic suppliers whenever possible, and her artisans were local women, but if the most beautiful lace in the world was made in France, that's where she would buy lace. Sharon accepted American Giant's strictures with equanimity, however. She called it "a reverse way of working," meaning that you used what you had and were resourceful around that.

Labor costs further limited what American Giant could design and sell. I noticed that although it made jeans, the label didn't make a jean jacket. Nor did it offer a popular variation, a sherpa-lined trucker jacket. Nor a five-pocket, quilted field coat, another staple of American sportswear. Why not? I asked Sharon. "Because all the money would go into the sewing," she explained. "When there's a lot of stitching needed on the garment, it obviously costs more." Levi's could sell its sherpa-lined jacket, made in Sri Lanka, for around $80. For American Giant to make the same coat and turn a profit, it would have to charge $400—way too much for the mid-priced consumer. Bayard expected to sell the flannel shirt, should he pull it off, for around $115, the upper limit of what he felt was reasonable.

Sharon's creative solution was to design clothing that was simple and beautiful and made of great fabric, but without a lot of tricks. No flat-felled seams. No adjustable waist tabs with buttons or other adornments that required a lot of stitchwork. American Giant's chore coat came unlined, with a single chest pocket; multiple pockets and a lining were too great an extravagance. "You open the fridge in America and make what you can from the ingredients you have in this fridge," Tam Ravenhill, who worked closely with Sharon and the design team to produce the garments, told me matter-of-factly. Now, with flannel, Sharon had to create a beautiful, appealing product from an empty fridge.

One afternoon, Sharon went shopping in Haight-Ashbury, searching for inspiration in vintage stores. She picked through piles of old plaids from the golden era of American clothing and bought her favorites: a shirt by Wrangler along with another flannel, made by an obscure workwear brand, that had a good weight to the fabric. The most beautiful in Sharon's eyes were 1970s-era flannels by Pendleton, the Oregon clothier. Made of pure virgin wool, with a hand-loomed look, the shirts were a harmonious merging of factory production and craft. "Super fluffy and gorgeous and, you know, brushed and soft and heavier," Sharon gushed. "Then the plaid, the actual design, is simpler and not too busy."

Back in her design studio, with its mood boards and shelves of sample fabric, Sharon laid out the shirts on a worktable for Bayard to inspect. Despite having no design training, he had a close hand in the creation of every garment. Initially, they pretended there were no limitations; they simply responded to what they liked. A vintage flannel with a simple graphic pattern quickly became their favorite inspiration. Sharon scanned the shirt into Photoshop and began creating numerous variations of the plaid pattern.

Eventually, reality set in. Someday, if American Giant succeeded in reviving flannel and the supply chain necessary to produce it, they might make a ten-color plaid like that of those gorgeous Pendletons. Something that Neil Young would have worn on a vinyl album cover. But presently, they had to be practical about what the reduced state of American manufacturing could manage, and what American Giant could afford. Baby steps. Sharon, Bayard, and James consulted on the phone. Ultimately, they settled on six yarn colors. From this palette, Sharon would design three colorways. "I want to create an indigo-based one that goes well with denim," she said. "I want a black-and-white one that looks a little Kurt Cobain-y. Then I want a toasty, warm, brown-based pattern that will go with traditional chinos."

However, there was an additional constraint put in place by James, intended to minimize costs and not overcomplicate the warping and weaving. Each pattern could feature no more than four of the six colors. Even that might be too ambitious. What if James came back and said his millworkers couldn't weave Sharon's patterns? "We might have to take it down from four to three," she said with acceptance.

❦ ❦❦❦ ❦

In May 2018, Bayard and James met for lunch at a chain sandwich shop in Manhattan's Garment District. I joined them at a back table, listening as they went over the "battle plan," as Bayard put it.

James was a tall, trim man with light brown hair, an impish smile, and heavy-lidded eyes. With a collared dress shirt, crisp jeans, and the kind of fleece vest favored by finance guys, he didn't seem the tatty flannel sort, but, he said, "I went to a few more Grateful Dead shows than I care to admit in college. I spent four or five years touring. It was me and my flannel. You had your khaki shorts, your Birkenstocks, and your flannel." He smiled. "And you had to have your shades. Especially when you went home after three weeks on the road."

At lunch, James spoke to Bayard and me in technical terms about flannel and why dyeing yarn was such a complicated engineering process.

"Were you concerned about functional machinery?" Bayard asked.

James shook his head. "I knew the machinery was still available. It was the expertise, the artistry. Getting your colors to come out exactly how your designer wants it. Flannel is an art and an art form."

One of Cotswold's obscure revenue streams was making yarn-dyed fabrics for uniforms for transit workers. On New York's Metro-North and Long Island Rail Road lines, the conductors wear a pinstriped shirt—a yarn-dyed, woven shirt. "It's not a sportswear product," James said. "It's a commercial product that is heavily synthetic. But I knew that I wasn't completely in the dark."

This was how tenuous the supply chain was for flannel. A rail worker's uniform had given them hope.

James told Bayard that he had lined up a firm to dye the yarn. The workers behind Burlington Manufacturing Services, or BMS, were yarn specialists. James called them "the best people I know."

Each point along the production chain was a hurdle to overcome, a test to be passed. Failing at any one of those points would sink the project. As tricky as dyeing was, James said he was most concerned about the warping stage, in which the thousands of dyed yarns were loaded onto a beam and prepared for the loom. It's "the hardest technical engineering aspect of this entire adventure," he said. "And it hasn't been done in thirty years."

BMS would be doing the warping as well, James said.

"When is this happening?" Bayard asked.

"Right now. Literally right now. The pattern is on the warper this morning."

Bayard sat up in his seat, caught by surprise. "Today? I didn't know that."

"We could have made a mistake with the yarn," James told Bayard. "You're not going to know it until you see it. We'll know if we passed the hurdle of warping by Wednesday next week."

Despite the note of caution, James looked upbeat, even confident. Until now, his career in textiles had traced a quarter-century race to the bottom, a competition to see who could make a product the cheapest. It had been one endless scramble to keep the family business going. But since Bayard had called, James had been thinking about more than just survival. "Now, for the first time, because of this collaboration, you get up in the morning and you've got a hop to your step," he told me. "Let's go make something awesome! I know we can do it again."

He looked to Bayard as if to a teammate in the huddle and added, "You get tired of always playing defense. *Let's play some offense!*"

◦ ◦◦◦ ◦

In June, now just five months to the deadline, Bayard traveled to the Carolinas to check up on production. I met him on a rainy weekday morning in the lobby of the Sheraton Raleigh. Although Bayard no longer shopped at Goodwill, his style had not evolved far. He wore the same outfit every time I saw him: American Giant blue jeans and a black cotton American Giant T-shirt. He approached briskly, greeted me with "Hey, dude," and turned toward the revolving door like we were already late. ("Never travel with Bayard," his wife had warned me. "He doesn't like a wasted minute. Inefficiency drives him crazy.")

Bayard's first meeting of the two-day business trip was with BMS, the yarn dyer that James had brought into the project. The firm's plant was in Burlington, North Carolina, an hour east of Raleigh. I drove the rental car while Bayard chatted away in the passenger seat. He was an engaged, intimate conversationalist, speaking in a voice that often sounded hoarse, as if from excessive talking at high volume. Five minutes into the drive, he revealed to me that he took cold showers each morning. "I read an article in the *Times* about it," Bayard said. "The writer basically said, 'Yeah, maybe there are health benefits, but the real benefit is you start the day with something that's hard.' It sets you up for a whole day of *I gotta get stuff done.*"

The conversation turned, as it often did when Bayard and I were together, to how deindustrialization had hollowed out America's heartland. The subject was appropriate to the setting: in just the five-year period between 1997 and 2002, North Carolina had lost 170,000 textile and apparel jobs. In 2003, the Kannapolis-based bedding manufacturer Pillowtex closed all sixteen of its plants in the U.S. and Canada, creating one of the worst mass layoffs in the state's history. Almost five thousand men and women were plunged into the abyss of the service economy to work part-time hours with no benefits at a dollar store or to pack boxes in a fulfillment center. Back in the Mission storefront days, Bayard had been reluctant to play up in marketing the fact that American Giant's clothing was all "made in the U.S.A.," or to talk politics. He believed that where the clothes were produced should be secondary to their quality. And he worried about getting lumped in with the flag-wavers and talk radio patriots, about appearing "bluntly patriotic," despite the bluntly patriotic name he had given his company.

Bayard was no conservative crusader. Yet as Americans everywhere grew angrier and more outspoken about the country's problems, and as Donald Trump brought the debate on trade with China front and center during his presidency, Bayard began to proselytize on behalf of the industry, trying to create not just good clothes but a movement. He met with Washington lawmakers who said they wanted to bring back manufacturing jobs, and when they failed, in his eyes, to follow through, he called them "completely full of shit." He wrote editorials chastising not just Big Apparel but Big Pharma and Big Tech, too, for "chasing cheap." I was not the first journalist to visit him in North Carolina—over the years, he had marched reporters and executives of competing apparel brands through the cotton fields and factories that supplied American Giant to show them that, yes, you could still make clothes here.

Bayard's politics and the source of his anger—the force of it— were hard to pin down. His indignation came across as genuine; he'd founded a company committed to U.S. manufacturing, after all. But having never worked in a factory himself, or lived in a factory town, his view of it was romantic and a little blinkered. The American Giant office staffers in San Francisco enjoyed free wellness programs and were treated to guest speakers and other perks. It had not occurred to him to do the same for the millworkers at the two sewing plants in North Carolina. When he caught himself and tried to correct the oversight, he was at a loss for what the employees of a rural factory might want, suggesting maybe a gym membership. There was an airy, rhetorical quality to his speech that sounded different from ground-up experience. "Lately, my thinking around free trade is . . ." he would opine, and go on to list his policy prescriptions, as if he were running for political office.

On the drive to Burlington, I heard for the first time what amounted to Bayard's stump speech, which he delivered time and time again to reporters, to elected officials, to industry colleagues, to his employees, to his family members including his eldest brother, Jay, who had followed in the Winthrop family tradition, attending Harvard, living in Greenwich, and running a wealth-management firm. (Jay had also invested in American Giant.) The stump speech blasted companies that made a "Faustian bargain" to save pennies per garment. It listed the benefits of doing business in the United States, how you could develop working relationships based on a common culture and something more than dollars and cents—true partnerships. The speech carried a note of optimism, suggesting a change was in the air. "There's no reason a lot of the big brands couldn't return to doing some of their production domestically and have a real impact," Bayard said. "And I think, by the way, this is happening." But it also warned of a deepening division in onshore manufacturing "between businesses that have the know-how, the vision, and the courage to invest and stay ahead of the curve, and those that don't."

It was raining lightly when we arrived in Burlington, a former textile manufacturing hub of fifty-eight thousand people that seemingly had yet to recover from the loss of its main industry. The

GPS took us through an empty business district and into a residential neighborhood of small bungalows with peeling paint and weedy yards and not a soul in sight. The area grew more industrial as we crossed a railroad siding and drove past a cement plant surrounded by a chain-link fence. We stopped for a red light at an intersection. On our left was an isolated row of brick storefronts—a bar, a Mexican restaurant, a tax preparer—all dark at midday. On our right, looking huge and eerily still—almost mirage-like through the windshield—was a massive textile factory.

We turned and drove slowly down a street that ran parallel to the building. It seemed to stretch on for half a mile. At about the halfway point, the facade was set back to accommodate a parking lot, and overlooking the lot were glass windows of what looked like offices. Hardly any cars were in the lot, so we drove right up to the door. A sign—CS INDUSTRIAL COMPLEX, with BMS listed as a tenant—confirmed this was the right place, but Bayard appeared doubtful. There were no signs of activity, no sounds of industry coming from inside the factory. Bayard stood in the parking lot in the drizzly rain. For once, he wasn't charging forth.

"I guess this is it," he shrugged before opening the door and going inside.

❦ ❦❦❦ ❦

They stood on the dirty carpet in the small lobby, with big smiles and arms extended for handshakes. The brain trust of BMS—Al

Blalock, Bill Singleton, and Ron Farris. The "best people I know," as described by James McKinnon. They ushered Bayard into a windowless room—drop ceiling, fluorescent lights, office furniture of the cheapest kind—and took their seats around a conference table.

"Welcome to BMS, a division of Decorative Fabrics of America," said Al, who was president of the company. He was short and trim, about seventy, with a downturned mouth and a tightly wound manner.

"Just a little bit about who we are, where we came from," Ron, the company's sales rep, chimed in. Ron had thick steel-gray hair and a leisurely, amused way of speaking, as if all of life was a sales call over a barbecue lunch.

"Yep, yep. Great, great," said Bayard in a clipped tone. I knew he loathed small talk and sales pitches.

Al sorted through some printed materials spread before him on the table. He looked displeased. "Our graphic artist could have done better. Goddammit," he muttered. He seemed to forget that Bayard was sitting there. Then he caught himself. "And, uh, okay. Our total company is made up of four divisions. . . ." He named them, explained what each one did. The company owned an upholstery fabrics plant elsewhere with three different businesses in that facility; the fourth division, BMS, dyed yarn in this massive factory.

"There's a historical marker out front," Al continued. "You may have seen it when you came in. This plant you're in, the Pioneer Plant, was built in nineteen twenty-three. It's been in operation ever since. It was the first Burlington Industries plant. You don't know Burlington Industries, but when I joined them in nineteen seventysomething, they were *the* largest textile company in the world."

At this, Bayard's ears perked up. "When were you the largest?" he asked. "At what point in time?"

"Seventies. Even into the eighties," answered Ron, who had also worked for Burlington. "Eighty-eight is when the crap kind of hit the fan."

The story, as the three men told it, was a parable of late-stage capitalism. "We had a hostile takeover by a private-equity corporate vulture," Al said. The corporate raider was Asher Edelman, who was an inspiration for the greed-is-good financier Gordon Gekko in the 1987 film *Wall Street*. During the '80s, many U.S. textile companies made large capital investments to stay competitive in the global market. Burlington, for instance, spent $40 million to replace a turn-of-the-century mill with a brand-new plant filled with the latest Japanese-made Nissan looms. The capital expenditures lowered Burlington's net earnings and caused the stock to "underperform," in the language of Wall Street. Edelman believed he could squeeze more profit from the company if he owned it. Management refused to sell it to him. The parties got into a bidding war over the stock, sending the price skyward.

The battle for Burlington dragged on for months, very publicly, until management succeeded in taking the company private through a leveraged buyout that left it saddled with $2.4 billion in debt. Burlington's first major decision after the LBO was to lay off five hundred employees and close the R & D division. In the following years, chunks of the company were sold off to service debt. Plants and divisions were closed and generous employee benefits were stripped back. As the broader industry continued to decline, Burlington cannibalized itself to stay afloat.

"I mean, we had our own roofing company, our own trucking company," said Ron, who had gone to work for Burlington right out of college, in 1979, when the company had more than a hundred and forty plants across fifteen divisions and some eighty-thousand employees worldwide. "Totally self-sufficient. And pretty much at that time all domestic."

In 2007, Burlington sold off its oldest asset, the Pioneer Plant. A retired company executive bought the building and formed BMS to keep the dyehouse going. Al, who had been a top boss at Burlington, was hired to run the new enterprise. Ron came aboard that same year after his division of Burlington—Home Decorative Fabrics, for which he supervised quality control—was sold to a competing firm. As for Bill, a big-bellied man with a deep, phlegmy voice, he had followed his father into the textile mills and worked in one Southern plant or another for forty-five years. For a span of those years, Bill had managed a dyehouse for J. P. Stevens, the company whose brutal hostility toward unions had inspired *Norma Rae*. He had to carry a card in his pocket printed with responses he was to give to any talk of unionizing.

"We've all lived through the downsizing of textiles," Ron said.

That much was apparent. They were rattling around a 650,000-square-foot factory practically by themselves, like the last survivors in a disaster film.

Nodding to his colleagues around the table, Bill said, "There's probably a hundred and twenty years of experience right here."

Getting back to the presentation, Al rummaged among spools of fabric on a nearby table, found a thickly braided rope, and held it up. "We do this yarn for the military. It's a forty-six-thousand de-nier polyester. This is propelling rope to go out of a helicopter."

"You ever see the movie *Black Hawk Down?*" Bill said to Bayard. "That's the ropes the marines used."

Bayard grabbed another spool. "What's this?"

"It's for a local gentleman who does hunting socks," Ron said.

The firm's other accounts included dyeing high-visibility yarn for safety vests, cotton-poly material for U.S. Air Force shirting, cord-ing for marching band uniforms, yarn for terry-cloth towels sold at the Masters Tournament, and parachute attachment lines for a client up in Rhode Island. "You get my drift about doing a lot of dif-ferent things?" Al said. "Let's say you're a specialist in polyester. Well, that doesn't mean squat because you're competing with the world. A company across town had only big dyeing machines and one or two types of products. And they're out of business as of this May."

In fact, BMS had not only dyed the yarn for American Giant but also handled the warping, too—the Pioneer Plant had that capabil-ity. Al riffled through the papers in front of him, coming up with printouts of the three patterns that Sharon had designed. He showed Bayard the sheets. "This is warp number one, this is warp number two, this is warp number three."

A look of alarm flashed across Bayard's face. He had entrusted James to oversee the critical warping stage, and James had delegated the job to these three doddering fellows and this ancient factory? What had he gotten himself into?

"So the beams will go down to Central?" Bayard reassured himself, referring to Cotswold's mill in South Carolina. "Central will weave it?"

"That's right," said Ron. "Matter of fact, they're down there now."

"Any problems there, Ron?"

"No. Actually," Ron said, reclining in his chair, "it went pretty well."

◦ ◦◦◦ ◦

Al, Bill, and Ron led Bayard on a tour of the plant. One had the sense of entering the bowels of a great ship—the murky light, the subterranean feeling, the distant rumble of heavy machinery. The workrooms had the vast dimensions of airport hangars, one cavernous space flowing into the next.

In one of the workrooms, yarn was being prepared for weaving. Eight "section beams"—huge steel rollers—sat on iron tracks. Each beam had a thousand ends of white yarn wound around it. A motor was unspooling all the yarn from the eight section beams and transferring it onto a single, even larger "loom beam" about twenty feet away. The process was a scene of unexpected beauty: thousands of white yarns, suspended in midair, flowing together as one body, like a fast-moving, translucent river.

Al, Ron, and Bill showed Bayard into the plant's color lab, a clean, white, brightly lit room walled off from the industrial workspaces. Bayard was introduced to Ron McBride, the plant manager, who had supervised the yarn dyeing for American Giant's flannel. A stocky man with glasses and a dusting of white in his red beard, McBride could also date his career back to the 1970s, when right out of high school he took a job in a color lab in Salisbury, North Carolina. He fell in love with textiles and shade matching then and there, he said, and decided to make it his career.

All around the orderly lab were clear glass bottles filled with chemicals marked "Soda Ash 100%" or "Common Salt 100%." Dye liquors were kept in plastic bottles on a rolling cart and labeled by color. Chemical formulas for various colors were written out on note cards organized in filing drawers. "What really caught me," McBride said, "was a dyer could look at a shade under a light box and say, 'This isn't quite right. I need to add five percent of yellow and eight percent of blue to make this piece of yarn look like it's supposed to look.' I thought it was amazing. It makes you feel good to take something that's not correct and fix it."

Al, Bill, and Ron brought Bayard out to another workroom behind the color lab that held several dyeing tanks spaced apart on a stained cement floor. Even if you'd never been inside a textile factory, it was obvious that the machines, like so much of the plant, were out of date.

"Nineties vintage," Al said, quickly adding, for Bayard's reassurance, "but thick stainless steel and, basically, they never wear out. We do one hundred thousand pounds a week here on these machines."

Bayard did not look reassured. The more he had seen of the BMS operation, the more his face had taken on a look of quiet panic. In the car earlier, speaking of the flannel project but also referring to American Giant more broadly, he had told me, "It's important that we've got people that are planning to be in the fight in five or ten years." BMS had the appearance of a company that might not be around in five or ten weeks.

In each enormous room, there were only one or two workers

walking around. Some rooms had no workers—only idle, inert machinery, like some Smithsonian exhibit on mid-twentieth-century manufacturing. The median age of the employees we did encounter was around sixty. It created a spectral feeling. I could imagine returning here later to find that everything we had seen had been an apparition, that the plant had really been silent and empty for years, as in a ghost story.

In the gloom of the dyeing room, Bill and Ron were kidding around with Bayard, pitching and flattering him like a couple of salesmen: "This is music to my ears, for you to come and say you want to make a product totally domestically." "That's an awesome feat." Bayard ignored the flattery, his face a constellation of worry. *My whole flannel program rests on these guys?*

Back in the parking lot after the tour, he looked like someone who'd emerged grimly into the daylight from a funeral home. "That plant and that team," he said as he got back into the car, "is not exuding a lot of innovation and investment and forward thinking."

When Bayard arrived the next morning at the Central mill, where the flannel fabric would be woven, James came smiling down the office hall to greet him.

Still rattled by his visit to BMS the day before, Bayard skipped the pleasantries. "Talk me off the ledge," he said. "Have you been to that facility?"

"Two years ago," James said.

"Well, maybe you should take another swing through. It just felt like a cavernous space where not much was happening."

James laughed. "That's the state of the U.S. textile industry."

Cotswold's Central mill appeared the opposite of the Pioneer Plant, alive on this hot summer day with the hum of machinery and the beeping of forklifts moving big bales of yarn. Tractor trailers with their rumbling engines pulled up to the loading dock outside to take finished goods coming out of the mill or drop off raw materials going in.

James showed Bayard into the wood-paneled office of Bill Steen, the vice president of manufacturing. Steen had been the plant supervisor of the mill when it was owned by Cannon Mills, more than thirty years before.

"What was this mill like back then?" Bayard asked.

"It was what we call an integrated mill," Steen said. "Bales of cotton, bales of polyester coming in one end, and when we shipped it out, it went out as fabric. When this was a Cannon plant, we had three hundred employees. Okay? Today, we have roughly a hundred on our payroll—and we're producing more yards than we were then."

The McKinnons had invested in the future and stayed ahead of the curve. The looms they'd inherited when they bought the mill in 1984 were all gone. And the looms they'd replaced them with had since been replaced, too. The electricity bill to operate the plant ran $150,000 a month in summer, Wink McKinnon had told me. But owning a mill gave Cotswold flexibility and control: it could make what it wanted when it wanted, rather than find itself at the whim of foreign factories or geopolitical curveballs.

James said to Bayard, "You have to be agile to survive in the textile business."

Steen held up the mill's production sheet for that week. "Look at that list. It must be thirty-five products we make here."

That week—the week of June 25, 2018—one of those manufactured products was flannel fabric for American Giant. They'd begun weaving it two days before.

James invited his partner to have a look. As he led Bayard from Steen's office out to the factory floor, James had a literal buoyancy about him. His springy walk bordered on a strut.

⦿ ⦿⦿⦿ ⦿

The weaving room lay behind a heavy steel door that slid on a track like the entry to a barn. A sign taped to it read "Please Keep Door Closed."

From the other side came a muffled rumble. James passed out earplugs. Then he gave a yank on the handle, and it was as if he had opened a door onto Niagara Falls.

The noise was deafening. It was not a monolithic wall of sound, though; it had discernible, earsplitting layers—a low base hum of white noise, a midrange of motorized grinding, a high register of sharp, fast, tinny stabbing. The noise leaped right inside your body and rattled your nerves after only a few seconds.

The source of the cacophony lay before us: 154 high-speed looms, about ten feet long by ten feet wide, placed in long rows in a room the length of about one and a half football fields, frantically jabbing away.

"PICANOL LOOMS! From BELGIUM!" James yelled over the roar. "Fastest today. Those looms cost about a hundred and fifty thousand dollars APIECE."

On this day, the mill's weaving room was almost entirely dedicated to making Cotswold's bread-and-butter product—a drab, off-white cloth destined to become curtains in hospitals, pocketing fabrics for jeans, and shirting fabrics for chefs and food service workers. But one loom, number seven, was weaving fabric whose plaid pattern stood out radiantly.

James made a "you first" motion to Bayard, who approached the square, boxy machine eagerly.

The rear of the loom held the warp beam, from which dyed yarns were unspooled. The crosswise weft yarns, meanwhile, were fed from spools on a nearby creel. This perimeter area was calm. The actual weaving took place in the machine's violent center. As the lengthwise warp yarns got pulled across the loom's surface, they passed through a wire heddle, which separated each one to allow for insertion of the crosswise wefts. Simultaneously, a reed, which resembled a big metal comb sitting atop the surface, moved up and down, guiding the yarns along. Meanwhile, down inside the machine's heart, a row of thin steel needles darted back and forth.

All these actions happened in furious, rapid coordination, and the effect was a kind of chaotic precision.

Rolling across loom number seven was one of Sharon's three patterns—the black, white, and navy plaid she'd designed to pair with jeans.

James smiled proudly.

Bayard hopped onto the operator's platform. He leaned over and put his face right down beside the furious needles to examine the woven cloth as it came through the loom. His expression registered first wonder, then approval, then, finally, a huge grin to match James's.

The gradients of color in the pattern, the variations in stripe width, the repeating grids—all exactly like Sharon's Photoshop renderings. Every last one of the 3,900 ends of yarn had been laid on the warp beam correctly. And the colors! The navy blue was deep and rich, like the twilight sky, with a uniformity of shade.

The old dogs at BMS had come through.

I thought back to Bill Singleton's remark about the hundred-plus years of experience collected in that plant, the talent gathered in that building to dye cloth. I learned later that Ron Farris had supervised quality control for a division of Burlington that produced two million yards of fabric per week. Ron McBride, who himself had run several dyehouses over a forty-year career, later told me that he'd been amazed at what the BMS guys could do when he went to work there. "With the equipment they had to work with," he said, "they produced phenomenal quality out of that plant."

Watching flannel cloth roll off the loom in a cascading sheet, Bayard couldn't stop grinning. For him and James, it was a shared moment of amazement. They had surprised even themselves.

James walked us away to a spot where he could talk without having to yell. "This plaid is *the* most technical product we have ever put in this mill," he said. "I wanted to challenge our ability. Could we do it?"

James confessed that there had been several false starts before

Bayard's visit. The blue and black weft yarns were so alike in color that James and his team had confused the spools. The first run had to be scrapped. Then they'd programmed the loom to insert the weft yarns in the wrong order. More frustration. So they'd tried a different pattern, but they couldn't get that one correct, either. It was only in the days before Bayard's arrival, working again with the black and navy plaid, that they'd finally figured it out.

But now that one pattern had been woven successfully, James was sure the hardest part was behind them.

"My confidence during this project has gone from ninety percent down to forty percent up to seventy," James said. "Now, it's at ninety-five."

Bayard was still watching the flannel cloth roll across the loom, in open-mouthed awe. "I'm happy for him," James said. "It's his vision."

Bayard came over to James. "Being able to look at the fabric and see that the depth of color and pattern are there . . . to see it come through so well . . . the color and depth and variation . . ." He was at a rare loss for words. Finally, he heaved a sigh of relief and said, "That's a load off."

· ··· ·

The summer deepened. To have flannel shirts on sale for Christmas, American Giant had to have finished—not just woven—fabric ready to be cut and sewn, at the absolute latest, by the end of September.

And then James ran into a problem he couldn't solve.

It was the napping. In July, Cotswold sent sample fabric to a finishing plant in North Carolina to be brushed and napped, and when it came back, well, it was something less than a cozy flannel.

"Let me show you what it looked like after our first pass," James said when I visited him one day at Cotswold's office near Manhattan's Bryant Park.

He left the room and came back carrying a six-foot-wide bolt of the black, white, and navy plaid. Unrolling the fabric across his desk, James invited me to feel it. I ran my hand along the surface. It had the coarse texture of cheap motel curtains, all the softness of outdoor carpet.

I remembered what John Bakane, the former Cone Mills CEO, had told me about flannel. How it required technicians—artistes—who could expertly set the napping machines and mechanics who could maintain them. How it was art, not science.

James shook his head. "Our finishing plant said, 'Hey, this is the best we can do.'" James sent the fabric back to the plant. Five times. Additional rounds of finishing yielded little improvement.

July flew by with no finished shirt, then August, then half of September.

Finding it difficult to explain over the phone the "pajama feel" that he and Bayard wanted, James sent the finishing plant detailed written instructions about the procedure. The plant manager told James that if they napped and brushed the fabric the way he wanted them to, it would become too brittle and break apart. What he was asking for, the finisher said, was impossible.

James began to freak out. He felt the whole project slipping away.

But he could only push the finishing plant so hard. "These guys, they were, like, 'You're talking about finishing five hundred yards. We finish *five hundred thousand* yards a day. Give me a break.'"

Throughout the ordeal, James was in regular communication with American Giant. At one point, he sent Bayard, Sharon, and Tam a sample of the coarse sample fabric so that they would understand what he was dealing with. By the middle of September, Bayard had lost his patience. He got James on the phone. "You're not going to make the deadline," he said.

With a heavy heart, James replied, "You're right."

At Cotswold's headquarters, James went into a postmortem of everything that had gone wrong. He had hired the finishing plant because it could do every part of the process under one roof. If he moved the fabric around too much, brushing it here, napping it there, preshrinking it somewhere else, he worried it would get screwed up. But he admitted his mistakes: "We tried to outsmart ourselves. It was a strategic sourcing error. It was a communication error. There were just so many things that went wrong."

On the phone with Bayard, James acknowledged they were now very unlikely to make their winter deadline. He apologized and took the blame.

"We have two options," James said. "We can scrap the thing completely and just call it a noble failure. Or we can continue on with the development and punt the whole thing another year."

But neither man was quite ready to give up.

In late September, in a last-ditch effort, James and Bayard sent a few rolls of fabric to Page Ashby at Carolina Cotton Works. CCW couldn't handle every process under one roof. That's why James hadn't gone to them first. Still, it had been Page who had collaborated with Bayard on the hoodie, agreeing to develop the fabric when other mills wouldn't. Without Page, there would be no American Giant. Could he nap the flannel?

Along with Bayard, I visited CCW's Gaffney, South Carolina, finishing plant, where industrial-scale washers and laundry presses vibrated and spewed steam into the air, bleaching and preshrinking fabric before it was made into clothes. The napping machine, by contrast, looked inert and primitive—a large square box with twenty-four rollers attached to a revolving cylinder. Each roller had little wires, like the bristles on a round hairbrush. Some were hooked and others straight.

There were three elements to operating the machine, Page explained. One was tension: the tightness of the fabric against the wires. The second was speed: how fast to turn each roller. The third was also speed: how fast to set the big cylinder that turned all the rollers.

The whole project came down to Page and CCW's napper operator—sixty-two-year-old Roger Putnam. A textile mill lifer, he had never napped flannel before. As Bayard put it, watching Putnam at work: "We succeed or fail on that man's shoulders."

Page, at least, showed no signs of worry. With easy confidence, he explained to me how he planned on making the flannel soft. "You have to raise those fibers out of the yarn. Get it to be a little bit fuzzy, if you will. Not make it like a blanket."

He smiled. "We just want to tickle it a little bit."

Later that fall, Page sent Bayard and James a sample. It had the soft pajama feel of the flannel shirt from Bayard's boyhood, the shirt that had made him feel cool and capable. CCW had tickled the fabric just right.

Another finisher, Yates Bleachery in Flintstone, Georgia, came aboard to handle the preshrinking. Then it would be on to Jade Apparel, a Philadelphia sewing factory run by a Vietnamese immigrant and her two daughters, for the final step: the sewing of the shirts.

Now that Bayard and James had successfully reassembled the entire supply chain, they came up with a new, modified plan. American Giant would do a limited run of a single pattern—two thousand yards of the black, white, and navy plaid, or enough to make twelve hundred shirts. BMS, Cotswold, CCW, Yates, Jade—all would have to rush production. But American Giant flannel would be available for Christmas, with more to come in the new year.

James directed his millworkers at the Central plant to focus exclusively on weaving flannel. He called Page's son Bryan and begged and pleaded for CCW to nap the first run of five hundred yards, a job that would normally take a month due to the plant's production schedule but that Bryan agreed to do in forty-eight hours.

Cotswold had worked with Yates Bleachery for thirty years, and it was because of that relationship that Tim Harris, Yates's general manager, stayed at the plant until 2:00 a.m. one night to finish the job.

James had just received an email from Harris, confirming the final inspection of the fabric when, on the morning of November 7, I dropped by his office.

"Yesterday at one twenty-four. That's when I knew. Mission complete."

Freed from the stress of deadlines, forgiven for his earlier failure, James was in an upbeat, philosophical mood. "Look at all of the energy and the brainpower and the people throughout North Carolina, South Carolina, and Georgia that really put their heart and soul into something that hopefully is a piece of art, a piece of beauty," he said.

With real emotion in his voice, he concluded, "It means something for all of us."

Not long after, a package arrived at my apartment in Brooklyn. The return label read "American Giant, San Francisco." Inside was a black, white, and navy flannel shirt. It practically glowed in my hands. The struggle of its creation was inseparable in my mind from the shirt itself, and it hung in my closet for weeks, unworn. I was afraid to wear it, fearful that if I carelessly ripped it or got a food stain on the front, there would never be another one.

"Woven and Made in USA," the neck label said.

When Bayard was next in New York for business, we met at a coffee shop. Was it worth it? I asked him. Was it worth all the time, energy, and resources?

"What I continue to be struck by is this undercurrent in the supply chain of 'Give us a shot,'" Bayard said.

At this, I thought of the BMS guys, sitting in the Pioneer Plant, waiting for someone to come along and hire them so they could dye beautiful cloth. I thought of James, a businessman with energy and ideas in an industry on life support.

As if speaking not to me but to the executives and sourcing managers of every onshore apparel brand, Bayard added, "There's a bunch of incredibly capable, motivated people here. Before you think this can be done easier or faster or cheaper overseas, remind yourself of that."

His eyes flashed.

"It's worth it for that alone—to prove the ability to do it."

Chapter 8

Resilience

The sock gods don't let us be happy for long," Gina Locklear said. It was May 2019, and the state legislature of Alabama passed a near-total ban on abortion. Pro-choice groups organized an economic boycott of the state. A hashtag—#BoycottAlabama—gained traction on social media, and major news outlets picked up the story. Along with broiler chickens and Mercedes-Benzes, Gina's socks got caught up in the protest. Customers emailed her, wanting to know her position on abortion before they would buy from her. Gina didn't comment publicly—she wanted to leave politics out of it and sell to everyone—but the ban caused her stress and hurt sales.

That fall, she dropped the Little River line. She was trying to streamline her life and business, take some things off her plate. She hired a freelance designer, a woman who lived in New York who knew how to code sock patterns, a rare and specialized skill. That took some weight off Vance, whose Parkinson's was really slowing him down now. Gina was still driving from Birmingham to Fort Payne every week, leaving early Monday and getting home late

Wednesday, driving back and forth between home and *home*. It was a balancing act, one she often struggled to get right.

It turned out to be a good thing that she'd cut out the second line, because a much bigger crisis was looming. Six months later, COVID hit.

The pandemic threatened both sides of the company, sales and manufacturing. On Instagram, Gina followed the boutiques that carried her socks, and she could see stores closing up in a panic, one after the other, from the West Coast to the Northeast. A lot of her wholesale orders didn't ship out in March, April, and May. No orders went out in June.

On the manufacturing side, suppliers closed. Gina got a call from her North Carolina cotton spinner, telling her they were shutting down for four weeks. The plant that dyed her yarn, also in North Carolina, halted operations as well. How could she make socks without yarn?

＊ ＊＊＊＊ ＊

In time, the critical shortages would extend to such items as ventilators, medicine, home appliances, semiconductors, cars, baby formula, and tampons. But they began with clothing.

In early March 2020, during the pandemic's first wave, hospitals and walk-in clinics across the country reported limited supplies of masks, gowns, gloves, eye shields, and other personal protective equipment, or PPE. In an internal memo, executives at Memorial

Sloan Kettering Cancer Center in Manhattan acknowledged that the hospital had just a week's supply of surgical masks for its health-care workers, several of whom had already tested positive for COVID-19. When a pediatrician in upstate New York tried to get masks for the employees of his eight-office physician group and called around to suppliers, he discovered that everything was on back order. On March 18, Dr. Stephen Anderson, an emergency physician at a hospital in the Seattle area, where the first U.S. case of COVID-19 was reported along with the first death, went on *Good Morning America* to let the nation know that he and his frontline colleagues desperately needed protective clothing. "I've got my mask for today right here, and I'm guarding it with my life," Dr. Anderson told host George Stephanopoulos, "because it could *be* my life."

A new term entered the public lexicon: N95. Few outside construction or ICU workers had previously heard of the respirator masks, which could filter out 95 percent of airborne particles, but now they were the single best thing to protect you from getting deathly sick. The demand for N95s was insatiable. Nurses and doctors were supposed to wear one mask per patient visit, then toss it for a new one. Across the country, that amounted to millions per day. And everyone else suddenly wanted an N95, or a stash of them. But the world's supply of PPE seemed to have mysteriously dried up. According to the supply-chain manager for Sloan Kettering, the hospital hadn't received a fresh shipment in a couple of months.

China made much of the PPE that American hospitals used, and since the initial outbreak of the virus in the city of Wuhan months earlier, the country had been stockpiling it. In the critical period before the rest of the world woke up to the seriousness of COVID,

China bought two billion masks from foreign countries, sucking up the global supply—much of which had been manufactured in China in the first place. The country also banned the export of new masks its factories produced (as would more than eighty other countries that produced them, including European Union members). As the United States clamored for medical supplies, China ramped up its awesome manufacturing capacity, not for American hospitals but for its own domestic needs. Daily production of surgical masks was around ten million at the beginning of February 2020; by month's end, Chinese factories were making more than a hundred million masks each day. And not just Chinese factories. The Communist government of Xi Jinping basically nationalized the factories of foreign companies, taking control of their workforces and production. A five-story building in Shanghai was a big N95 manufacturing facility for the American firm 3M. When a *New York Times* reporter showed up there in early March, a worker told him where all the masks were going: "They're being sent to hospitals in Wuhan."

The U.S. government maintained a Strategic National Stockpile, but the number of masks it held—twelve million N95s and thirty million surgical masks—amounted to 1 percent of the estimated three and a half billion masks needed to get the nation through one year of a pandemic. The stockpile also had inadequate supplies of gowns, gloves, face shields, test swabs, and ventilators. More than a month into the outbreak, with new cases and deaths rising sharply, there were stories of nurses washing and reusing the same masks for days, doctors wearing raincoats and snorkeling gear into emergency wards, an entire hospital floor with just a single gown.

In New York City, an early epicenter of the crisis, nurses at one hospital wore trash bags as protective gowns. A forty-eight-year-old nursing manager in the same hospital contracted the virus and died. With the city unable to get more gowns, Mayor Bill de Blasio put out a request to the New York Mets for rain ponchos. The solution seemed no less absurd than the one proposed by the Centers for Disease Control and Prevention, which said that in lieu of N95s, nurses and doctors could tie bandanas around their faces. During a protest by health-care workers outside a hospital in the Bronx, a young resident stood before the television cameras and said, her voice shaking, "Every day when I go to work, I feel like a sheep going to slaughter."

Americans watching such harrowing scenes on the news were asking the same question. Why were doctors and nurses at the best hospitals in the richest country in the world wearing trash bags to work?

⁕ ⸻ ⸰

The essential component of N95 masks—what keeps tiny virus droplets from getting into a person's throat and lungs—is a material called melt-blown nonwoven fabric. It is the same material found in disposable diapers and sanitary pads. Melt blowing is a complex manufacturing process in which polypropylene pellets are heated and stretched to create thin strands of plastic that can be made to form a dense mesh web. The layered material creates a filter through which air can pass but not particulates. If you don't control the manufacturing of this kind of material, you can't make the masks.

Just a few decades ago, most medical protective gear worn in America, like most apparel, was made in America. But big medical supply distributors started sourcing from overseas factories in Asia to lower their costs and drive up profits. The hospitals those firms sold to didn't stockpile the gear, because it was cheap to purchase and expensive to store. Just-in-time inventory methods, which move goods only as they are needed, had always delivered more. "We got focused on 'If we can save a penny, let's get it all done in one part of the world,'" Bob Riney, the president of health-care operations for Michigan's Henry Ford Health, told *The Detroit News* early in the pandemic.

In 2019, China produced nearly half of the world's melt-blown fabric, the U.S. around 15 percent. China also made the machines that could convert melt-blown textiles into wearable PPE. Prestige Ameritech, the largest U.S. maker of N95 masks, sourced its material from third parties. To manufacture melt-blown material itself was a big financial risk; one machine cost $5 million, and how could a U.S. company compete on price with China? Lydall, Inc., a Connecticut company that did manufacture melt-blown fabric, operated a single production line at the start of the pandemic. As bodies piled up in refrigerated trailers outside hospitals and the elderly died alone in nursing homes, the American Medical Association called on the Trump administration to establish a new Manhattan Project, to "leverage every tool at its disposal" to manufacture PPE and contain the spread of the virus. But America in 2020 was a very different country and economy than in 1942.

The Trump administration did award a combined $134.5 million to four companies—O&M Halyard, 3M, Honeywell, and Hollingsworth & Vose—to ramp up N95 production, but the masks wouldn't arrive for several months. Lydall would also receive a $13.5 million contract from the federal government to increase production, but a second production line wouldn't be up and running until the end of the year, and a third not until the following May. It didn't matter how much money the government threw at the problem. The wait to purchase a machine that could produce melt-blown fabric was by some estimates more than a year.

So, instead, Americans watched as the vice president pleaded for private construction firms to donate respirator masks to hospitals and health-care centers—and as the president's son-in-law orchestrated airlifts of masks, gloves, and gowns from Asia at an exorbitantly high cost to taxpayers and in coordination with the very same health-care companies that had outsourced their purchasing and production. In the meantime, ICUs were running out of beds, and by the end of April, more than one million cases of COVID-19 had been recorded in the country. Two thousand Americans were dying every day.

＊ ＊＊＊＊ ＊

Kim Glas was following the shortage of medical supplies like everyone else. Glas grew up in western New York, in the blue-collar town of Lockport, where General Motors' Harrison Radiator division plant shed thousands of jobs during the '80s and '90s through downsizing and automation. She came of age in that period of transition. Her family had lived in a '50s-style ranch house on a street where everyone lived in similar homes and worked at Harrison Radiator. But in the Lockport of her adulthood, poverty now ran so high that every student in the school district qualified for free breakfast and lunch. Glas had planned to become a social studies teacher, but instead, she thought, *I need to be helping my community. I need to be in Washington, D.C.* She worked for a local congressman, John J. LaFalce, and when he retired, in 2002, she heard about a guy in northern Maine who drove a forklift at a papermill and had won a seat in the 108th Congress. She spent a decade as a staffer for that guy—Mike Michaud—working on Capitol Hill on issues of manufacturing and trade policy. Now, at forty-four, Glas was president of the National Council of Textile Organizations, or the NCTO, the largest textile industry trade group.

In mid-March, she read an article in *Politico* about the shortage of lab materials for COVID-19 test kits. She had a friend who knew Peter Navarro, the director of trade and manufacturing policy for the Trump administration. She asked the friend, "Can you get word to the White House that I might have somebody who can make swabs?" That was how, hours later, Glas came to be on a conference call with the friend, Navarro, and Andy Warlick of Parkdale Mills, the North Carolina textile manufacturer.

In addition to its yarn-spinning division, Parkdale owned U.S. Cotton, which was the world's largest manufacturer of cotton swabs, producing more than nine billion a year. Andy, like Glas, thought Navarro was going to ask him to make cotton swabs, to which he could have replied, "How many million do you want by next week?" Instead, Navarro said, "I need masks."

The White House was looking for every type of mask—N95s, surgical masks, and reusable cloth options to offer people some measure of protection. Navarro wanted to know if the U.S. textile industry could make the reusable cloth kind on a quick turnaround. They would go into the strategic stockpile and then be distributed in coordination with FEMA to local communities across the country. "How many masks do you need?" Andy asked. Navarro told him: six hundred million.

Under the leadership of Andy's late father-in-law, Duke Kimbrell, Parkdale had grown from a one-mill operation in the 1960s into the largest cotton-yarn spinner in North America, with more than a dozen plants in eight states. Duke had started in the mill sweeping floors after school. He went on to serve in World War II, and after the war he used the G.I. Bill to get a degree in textiles at North Carolina State. When he orchestrated a leveraged buyout and became owner, in 1983, he kept the company private, which meant that he could pump money back into the operation without worrying about boosting the stock price to please shareholders. Parkdale automated its plants before its competitors. It developed relationships with Japanese and German textile machine manufacturers to install the most efficient, automated machines in the world. Through cost savings and efficiency, the company took business from other rivals. When Andy joined Parkdale from a job at Milliken, in 1984, he focused on operational systems, doubling down on innovation and quality. In the following decades, Parkdale got stronger, faster, and even more competitive, becoming one of the last big U.S. textile firms standing.

Since yarn was the first input in making clothing, Andy knew everyone down through the supply chain. He hung up with Navarro and started calling around to his contacts, putting together a coalition: *Are you on board? How much volume can you do?* Andy's son, Davis, a vice president, and an executive named Charles Heilig worked on the logistics. Within forty-eight hours, Andy got back to the White House. Yes, the industry could do it. The coalition committed to make six hundred million masks in ninety days.

The pandemic was revealing a striking truth: the companies best able to help their fellow Americans during this crisis were the ones that still had factories in America. This was true not just of Parkdale's coalition but also across the apparel industry: New Balance retooled two of its shoe plants to produce medical face masks. Though Carhartt now made most of its clothing overseas, it still operated four cut-and-sew facilities in Tennessee and Kentucky, which would produce more than two million surgical masks and fifty thousand gowns, the company said. Other companies had less effective responses. Gap, for instance, announced a plan to get masks, gowns, and scrubs to frontline workers through its factory partners—code for contract factories half a world away.

But if you were resourceful and knew how to sew, a nearly lost skill in a world of click-and-shop fast fashion, the home could become a factory. That spring, an army of home sewers across the country began making masks for their fellow citizens. They collected fabric, cut it up, and stitched it together to aid health-care staffers, police officers, EMTs, paramedics, and other frontline workers. The home sewers posted tutorials to YouTube for others to follow. Sewing groups with dozens of members sprung up to supply Riverside University Health System Medical Center in California and Allina Health's network of hospitals and clinics in Minnesota. The masks they produced weren't medical grade by any stretch—they were DIY designs, stitched together with a few layers of cotton, elastic straps, and maybe an insert cut from a coffee filter.

Jovanna Porter, a sewer in rural Pennsylvania making masks for her niece, a doctor working in a coronavirus ward in New York, used the twist ties from garbage bags to form nose bridges. Krystal Douglas, the owner of Music City Sewing in Nashville, repurposed the elastic from her bra straps to make her mask bands. Michele Hoaglund, the owner of Treadle Yard Goods, a fabric store in St. Paul, gave away mask-making kits to more than two hundred people who showed up at her store. Each kit contained a pattern and enough material to make two dozen. Hoaglund was happy to do her part but angry, too. An army of home sewers using leftover fabric scraps? It was a throwback to the 1918 flu epidemic. "It should never have come to this," Hoaglund told *The New York Times*. "We're doing what the federal government should be doing."

As for the Navarro-led project, what remained of the domestic textile industry pivoted overnight to making masks. The Warlicks and one of their largest customers, Hanesbrands, helped coordinate the coalition of industry competitors. Hanesbrands leveraged their expertise in design to create tech packs, and their logistics department coordinated delivery. Other Parkdale customers such as Fruit of the Loom, Beverly Knits, and SanMar joined the effort. (Parkdale was also participating in other PPE programs at the same time, converting production lines to make polyester fiber for the tips of testing swabs and spinning specialized yarn for gowns.) One cut-and-sew shop would contract out to another cut-and-sew shop, the work trickling down from the big players to the little guys. Factory owners heard about the project and reached out to Glas or the Warlicks: *I've got a hundred sewers in the Garment District in New York. How do I get involved?* They were eager to answer the call to action, and they also saw a way to avoid laying off their workers at a time when the whole economy had ground to a halt. It seemed like the entire U.S. textile supply chain was working on the mask program.

Hundreds of companies ended up participating. They worked for Hanes, SanMar, Beverly Knits, or Parkdale. The consolidation allowed a wide network of suppliers to participate while limiting the number of contracts the federal government would have to deal with. The participants charged the government less than seventy-five cents per mask. A few manufacturers chose to opt out because they could make masks on their own and net a lot more profit—it was a time of rapacious price gouging. "I didn't want that in our coalition anyway," Andy said. "I wanted 'We're Americans, and we're being called on.'" One of the companies that answered Andy's call was American Giant.

● ●●●● ●

Since the start of the outbreak, American Giant's revenues had fallen off a cliff. Online sales, which made up the bulk of the business, were down 50 percent through mid-March. The retail stores in San Francisco, New York, and Los Angeles were closed until further notice because residents in those cities were under orders to shelter at home. Civilization was collapsing—who was buying a hoodie, anyway?

Of pressing concern for Bayard Winthrop was the money that American Giant owed to its suppliers—finishers like Carolina Cotton Works, denim mills like Mount Vernon—for purchase orders already made. He also had forty-five employees who were relying on a paycheck to support their families. The pandemic was a trial by fire for business leaders; a shutdown of the global economy was unprecedented, and some businesses weren't going to make it through. It was entirely possible that American Giant would be one of the casualties.

Unable to go to the office, Bayard led a companywide call every morning at nine with his furloughed retail employees, the corporate staffers in the Bay Area, and the supervisors of the two sewing mills in North Carolina. Everyone but the supervisors and the seamstresses at those mills was working from home. He talked while doing laps around Fort Scott in the Presidio with his dog, amped up on caffeine and the drama of the moment.

"We're in a fucking tornado right now," he told them.

He turned out to be a good leader in a crisis. He didn't panic and stayed optimistic—in his gut, he believed COVID to be a temporary disruption. He didn't try to project false confidence. He was honest and up front with people. The company promised to pay the furloughed retail employees through March, with no guarantees after that. Cash was everything right now. The situation shifted day-to-day. If things got worse, the company would have to start looking at layoffs in production, marketing, design—basically everywhere.

Bayard's partners in the storm were Kent Kendall, his childhood friend and COO, a soft-spoken moral compass within the company, and Pete Dinh, the forty-eight-year-old CFO. Pete and his parents and seven siblings had come to the United States from Vietnam as "boat people." After the fall of Saigon in 1975, like other refugees the family had piled into an overcrowded fishing vessel, which drifted in the South China Sea for weeks until a South American freighter spotted it. Pete was three. The Dinh family ended up in Philadelphia, where Pete's father started over with a job in the housekeeping department at Bryn Mawr Hospital, and Pete and his siblings worked hard and excelled in school, in the tradition of first-generation immigrants. Pete got a scholarship to a prep school in the suburbs, then got into Stanford to study economics, which brought him out to the Bay Area. Due to his background, he had a cautious streak, especially around money, and a methodical approach that made him the exact person you wanted beside you in a crisis.

Bayard and Pete sat in a room for a day and came up with a doomsday plan. The goal was to buy the business enough time to allow sales to recover.

The first thing they did was call all their suppliers to see how many orders could be canceled, delayed, or partially paid. Going forward, any purchasing of raw materials would be made by senior leadership only: Bayard, Kent, or Pete. Having found they had some leeway with their suppliers, they turned to operational costs. They cut every unnecessary expense: travel, entertainment, services for an office that was sitting empty. But with such weak sales, that wasn't enough to keep the business going.

Finally, they looked at payroll. If senior management took pay cuts for several months, they could prevent layoffs for that period. Bayard volunteered to take a 50 percent cut to his compensation— Pete had to convince him not to waive his entire salary—and Pete and Kent took substantial cuts as well. "If the business continued to deteriorate beyond that period," Pete said, "all bets were off."

As dire as it was for American Giant, in some ways the company was in a stronger position than big apparel brands with global supply chains. Bayard and Pete were dealing with U.S.-based suppliers who were operating under the same set of rules and circumstances. The owners of those businesses had become true partners—in some cases, friends. Bayard could get on the phone to Bryan Ashby at CCW—as he did in late March—and say, "I know we owe you six hundred and fifty thousand, but can one hundred and fifty get you through for a bit?" A foreign factory owner they barely knew might not be so accommodating. Big apparel brands that manufactured overseas worked roughly a year in advance in their production schedules. The merchandise for next season—fall 2020—was probably already on a boat crossing the ocean, on its way to retail stores that were either closed or empty. Retailers would soon grow burdened by piles of unsold clothing, all of it seasonally dependent and destined to be heavily discounted or liquidated. By contrast, American Giant controlled its manufacturing and could be flexible in the moment. Bayard could call up William Lucas, the plant manager at the Middlesex factory, and tell him to make only what the company had orders for. Or to drop every product from the line but basic black T-shirts. Or to stop clothing production altogether because American Giant was pivoting to masks.

The call from Andy Warlick was the first sign that the business might weather the storm. Joining the coalition meant that the sewing plants could stay open as essential facilities, even if North Carolina enacted a shelter-in-place order, keeping the workers working. In late March, a note was posted to American Giant's Instagram account: "Effective today we are making masks and distributing them to the frontline medical personnel that are confronting this crisis. Our initial target is 35,000 per week, and we expect to be climbing aggressively from there. . . . We ask for your patience and understanding as we stop production of American Giant products in support of this effort. You may experience some out of stocks in the coming weeks, but we trust that you will understand. Right now we need masks more than sweatshirts!"

The mask project was good for morale—the employees felt they were helping in some small way in a moment of fear and powerlessness—and the government contract provided desperately needed revenue to boot. (Months later, many factory owners would tell Andy Warlick or Kim Glas that the mask program had saved them from bankruptcy.) Not that Bayard had joined the coalition for financial reasons. In truth, he'd wanted to play a vital role his entire career, and coming as it did now, it seemed to vindicate everything he'd been shouting for the past decade. While the only option of most bigger and more profitable brands was performative gestures—like the donation to coronavirus relief efforts Ralph

Lauren made through its corporate foundation—American Giant was able to act quickly to offer tangible assistance.

Another boost came one morning on the companywide call, after Sharon Aris chimed in with an idea. As Sharon told the group, she'd been working from home one day when, distracted during a long Zoom call, she began browsing through her grandmother's handwritten recipe journals from World War II. Her family had lived in Sunderland, on England's northeast coast, during the wartime years of the Blitz and food rationing. Sharon was struck by the resourcefulness of her gran's recipes, the way every single bit of everything was used. She began to think about how that creativity in a time of hardship could be applied to making clothes.

Every apparel brand that Sharon had ever worked for dumped its excess inventory, selling unused fabric and trimmings to jobbers and slashing the price of unsold garments to get rid of them. But American Giant, in its scrappiness and frugality, held on to leftover bolts of fabric and other raw materials, along with clothes that hadn't sold or had slight defects. It was all sitting on shelves in the back of the Middlesex factory. When Sharon started at the company, she'd asked a member of her design team to make an inventory list so she'd know they had two thousand yards of this or that fabric or six hundred zippers of a certain shade or type.

Now she told the group, "What if American Giant created a collection from all the inventory we have? Like cooking from what's in your pantry. Just like my gran, we shouldn't have anything sit and go rotten in the cupboards."

Everyone loved her idea, and very quickly, using the inventory list and CAD software, Sharon worked up a collection of the brand's signature hoodies. She used loud colors that clashed on purpose—firehouse tones of orange and red; army greens, olive, and taupe; safety-orange drawcords—making the mishmashed nature of the process a feature of the design. Some of the fabric had been hanging around since the company's beginnings. In the end, American Giant had about two thousand men's and women's hoodies that cost next to nothing to make and told the story of a company grinding to survive. The hoodies went on sale that fall as the Vault collection.

Sharon's grandmother's example rubbed off on the staff. As the weeks went by, it became a kind of game—how scrappy can we get? A stockpile of ribbed fabric was turned into a ribbed-shirt program so that the brand could offer new products even as it tightened the belt. When the factory ran out of white buttons and couldn't get more, ivory was used instead. There were some boxes of clothes in one-off seasonal colors that hadn't sold. For sixty cents a yard, the fabric could be dyed black by CCW, resurrecting dead inventory. There was no way Levi's or J. Crew could put sweatshirts meant to be sold that season back on a boat to Vietnam for re-dyeing.

✦ ✦✦✦ ✦

Economist and businessman Mohamed El-Erian, the current president of Queens' College, Cambridge, had foreseen the post-COVID world early on, and in a May 2020 essay he published in *Project*

Syndicate, he wrote that "the corporate world's multi-decade romance with cost-effective global supply chains and just-in-time inventory management" was effectively over. El-Erian, a skillful explainer of complex issues and a coiner of catchwords, went on CNBC and Bloomberg TV throughout the spring and summer to lay out the new paradigm under which companies needed to operate. The term he came up with was old hat to Andy Warlick, Sharon Aris, and every other person involved in making clothing domestically: *resilience*.

◦ ◦◦◦◦ ◦

One day in May 2020, Bayard was in his pickup truck driving around the Bay Area to drop off care packages with masks and thank-you notes for his employees. The terror of those first days and weeks of the pandemic had mostly subsided. American Giant's business had stabilized and even strengthened. Sales that month were tracking 50 percent above the year before. Add in the mask program, and Bayard was feeling increasingly optimistic.

He had noticed the beginnings of a rebound as early as the week that Tom Hanks got COVID and the NBA suspended the rest of its season, when it felt like the whole world was tipping on its axis. Bayard was trying to go easy with the marketing, to walk a fine line between recognizing that people were dying and needing to sell clothes. Amid all that confusion and fear, American Giant had sent out a promotional email about a track pant. Within fifteen minutes, the company saw an uptick in sales. It was odd. But in retrospect, it was the beginning of a profound shift in work life—the birth of the work-from-home economy. And the new work uniform was sweatpants and hoodies.

"We are the beneficiary of a bunch of factors it would have been hard to predict or plan for. We're in the category that people are buying," Bayard said, pulling up to Pete's house in the Richmond District.

By then, many apparel brands were in deep trouble. J. Crew, JCPenney, and Neiman Marcus had filed for Chapter 11. Gap had stopped paying rent on all its stores and said it wouldn't reopen some of them. The direct-to-consumer brands Rothy's, Everlane, and ThirdLove all announced layoffs and furloughs.

"Many businesses will perish," Bayard said as he hopped back in his truck and headed over to Oakland to deliver another care package. "Some will emerge stronger. We are determined to be one of them."

Going into the summer of 2020, American Giant was doing brisk business, and the problem now occupying Bayard's thoughts was how to produce more clothes, because the company had stopped buying raw materials when the pandemic hit. "We're sold out of sweatpants," he said. "We can't chase that business. We have no ability to make that shit right now."

Flush with government stimulus checks and stuck at home, Americans were going on online shopping sprees, buying sweatpants, hoodies, and other leisurewear. None of Bayard's employees lost their jobs that spring and summer, and by winter, he would be hiring to fill sev-

eral positions. American Giant seemed weirdly purpose-built to pros-
per during a global pandemic.

●━━●━●

Gina Locklear didn't turn to mask making—sock machines are
very specific, limited as they are to producing socks—but she, too,
came through the pandemic surprisingly well. After she got through
freaking out, she returned to her habitual state of shrewd resiliency.
You needed that quality to function in the field even in normal
times, so in a way, Gina was well prepared for this unprecedented
crisis. The cotton spinner and yarn dyer she worked with were small
family businesses like Emi-G. Together they would figure something out. "Everyone is going through the same situation," she told
herself. "And, honestly, we have it good because we make our own
socks." She was hearing that brands that manufactured in contract
factories overseas were dealing with huge supply-chain challenges.
At least she still had a stock of yarn. "We could make some adjust-
ments with our fall line in terms of colors if our suppliers don't open
right back up."

Her preexisting e-commerce platform was another silver lining.
As pandemic-era shopping shifted online, Gina noticed an uptick in
her sales. Countless media outlets, including fashion sites like *Refin-
ery29*, published articles about how to help small businesses during
the crisis. "People want to support not only businesses who make
their products in the United States but small businesses," Gina said.

"We feel that. We have very loyal customers—who we hear from—who want to make sure we keep making socks." Another thing she had going in her favor: socks are a cozy essential, an item people stock up on when they're sheltering. And, Gina reasoned, "I think the bright, happy patterns were a good thing, especially during that time. Someone actually told me that the brightness of our socks made them feel better when they looked at their feet." So loyal customers were ordering her socks, but she was gaining a lot of new customers, too. Christmas 2020 sales were surprisingly good, up almost 30 percent from the year before. The pandemic hadn't killed her business. It had made it stronger.

But just days into 2021, one of those time bombs that had been ticking in the background exploded.

Gina was in the kitchen at the mill, going over samples for Zkano's spring line, when Vance walked in. He'd just spoken to her parents. He repeated to Gina what he'd told them—he was putting in his notice.

At fifty-two, he went home after his shift each day and got straight into bed because he was so worn out from his Parkinson's. The time during the workday when he felt good was getting shorter and shorter. His mind wasn't as sharp as it used to be, and twice he'd fallen at work. That's what had prompted his decision. "I didn't get hurt or nothin', but I'm lucky I didn't," Vance told me when I visited Fort Payne again that May. "When you start thinkin' you might cause problems for the mill, it's time to move on."

The way Vance delivered the news, in a tone of finality, added to Gina's upset. Her whole face fell, and she burst out crying right in front of him. Vance said he would stay until December, giving the

Locklears almost a full year to find and train his replacement. But to the family—especially Gina—he was irreplaceable. She couldn't have started Zkano without him, and she didn't know how she could continue without him.

"It takes many, *many* years to gain the kind of knowledge that he has," Gina said. "You don't just put on a style that you've run before and think it's going to run perfectly. You might get a hole in the toe. You don't know why. Sometimes the machines run well, sometimes they don't. You just have to constantly figure that type of stuff out. And someone who doesn't know the machines well can *never* figure it out."

As she welcomed me into her office, Gina's face was a picture of worry, and her voice quavered. She sighed and brought up my first visit to Fort Payne, back in 2016 when she'd recently won the *Martha Stewart Living* award and everything was looking up. "Things were happy then," she said. "I'm in a place of stress right now."

The Locklears began the search for Vance's replacement. Terry called around to his hosiery friends, asking if there was someone still working in the mills who fit the bill, but he exhausted his leads pretty quickly. Gina heard about an organization called the Manufacturing Solutions Center, in Conover, North Carolina, which is part of Catawba Valley Community College. Its stated mission is to help U.S. textile manufacturers increase their sales and efficiency and find skilled workers. She called the center one day to pick an expert's brain about how to find a new tech. The person she spoke to told her, "My advice is you just keep the one you have."

Aside from Vance, she had another staffing crisis looming. The

New York–based freelance sock designer with whom Gina worked had told her she was looking for full-time employment. In an ideal world, Gina would have hired the woman permanently, but she couldn't afford to pay a big-city salary. It was only a matter of time before her designer would leave her, too.

For years, Gina had worried about orders drying up and putting her out of business. But now she worried about workers. And she realized that problem was more dire. You could create new business. You couldn't invent someone with thirty years of experience in the hosiery industry.

One day, Gina thought of the most accurate word to describe what it was like being a U.S. clothing manufacturer: *vulnerable.*

"We are all vulnerable," she said. "Even though we have all this business, we are vulnerable due to lack of skill set. It dawned on me this year. People leaving us could actually close us down."

The previous fall, Emi-G had hired a new line knitter and fixer named Barry. Barry's family had once owned and operated a mill out in the countryside, and he'd grown up in the sock business, like Gina. Although he'd been working for the Locklears for only a short time, they decided that Barry would replace Vance as production manager. For several months, until Vance left, Barry would apprentice alongside him. He would try to fill very big shoes.

Gina had reservations about Barry from the start, but she chalked it up to the fact that Barry wasn't Vance. In physical appearance and temperament, the two were opposites. Barry was in his late forties, with a ready smile and a clean-cut look that masked a combustible side to his personality. He was a chatterbox. He could talk socks all day long. Mostly about the machines. He'd go deep into the weeds, explaining each intricate moving part and its purpose. When I was first introduced to him in the knitting room, Barry held up his hand to show me a childhood scar that ran across the tops of his fingers. He said he got the scar as a young boy, when he was helping his dad package socks with a sealer iron that didn't have a cover over the heating wire. "The wire was set at three-hundred-something degrees, and it burned me right down to the bone," Barry said, almost proudly. "My sister, it burned her so bad it peeled her hand back a little bit. Her scar is wider than mine."

Through that spring, summer, and fall, Vance and Barry worked side by side. One time, an overnight storm knocked the power out and caused the air compressor that powered the Lonatis to shut down. The following morning, Vance and Barry had to reboot every machine. Barry took to the challenge of coding in Gina's patterns on the computer. Just like Vance, he found it intellectually engaging.

"He's willing to learn, and that's the main thing," Vance said.

Things were looking up. In November 2021, Gina was contacted by a producer from CBS News. The network wanted to send a crew down from New York for a segment about made-in-America products being so in demand during the pandemic, on account of the supply-chain crisis. Gina's sales proved it; 2021 was turning out to be Zkano's best year ever. The TV spot would be a big deal. The mill was buzzing with anticipation.

But on the day the film crew arrived, Barry showed up to work in a Trump T-shirt. He'd never worn anything with a political slogan before, but he seemed to want to make a statement to TV viewers. Terry asked him to please change his shirt. "We can't be political here," Terry said. Barry left—and never came back. They'd lost almost a year training him.

With six weeks until Vance was due to retire, Gina did what she always did—she dug down and persevered.

Kenny Young, the line knitter who worked for her parents, would take Vance's place, she decided. Kenny was forty-nine—not young but not retiring anytime soon—and he was from the Fort Payne of the old school. He'd started in the sock mills at fifteen and had worked for the Locklears going back to the Russell Athletic days. Kenny was steadfast and loyal, like Vance. Someone Gina had known since childhood.

And so Vance began a crash training course with Kenny. Six weeks later, in January 2022, after making socks for more than half his life, Vance Veal walked out of the mill to start his new life.

He stayed retired for two months.

After running through all his fix-it projects at home, Vance grew bored. He kept wondering what was happening over on Airport Road. He talked to Terry, and they worked out a deal. Vance would return a few days a week to help out part-time and continue training Kenny.

When Gina walked in one morning and saw Vance back in the knitting room, she burst into tears again. Tears of joy.

Chapter 9

New Lines

Not long after Bayard Winthrop had succeeded in reviving American flannel, I met with him at a coffee shop off Manhattan's Bryant Park. He burst through the door as usual, in no need of more caffeine. Lately, he told me, he had been considering moving American Giant's headquarters out of San Francisco to North Carolina. It would put the company in the heart of the U.S. textile industry, close to its factories and suppliers. We drank our coffee and talked about other things. After a few minutes, Bayard shifted in his seat restlessly, and I could tell that the internal motor that drove him was revving up again. He leaned across the table and said he had a new idea.

The idea was inspired by Jerry Hamill, a cotton farmer from Halifax County, North Carolina. Bayard had gotten to know him through his visits to the state. It was Hamill's farm to which he sometimes took journalists and apparel executives. Bayard said he wanted to make hoodies knitted from cotton grown on Hamill's land. The cotton would be spun into yarn at Parkdale's plant in Gaffney, made into garments at American Giant's sewing factory in

Middlesex, and dyed and finished at CCW or another nearby facility. The typical sweatshirt traveled many thousands of miles before it got to the person who wore it, Bayard said. This sweatshirt's production trail would stretch less than eight hundred.

It would be the clothing version of farm to table. Bayard already had a catchphrase for the concept. He called it "from dirt to shirt."

●　●—●　●

"Globalization is not something we can hold off or turn off. It is the economic equivalent of a force of nature, like wind or water." Bill Clinton had told that to an audience in Vietnam in 2000. Twenty years later, Americans had witnessed, first with disbelief and then with anger, the unpreparedness with which the country faced the COVID crisis. The images of nurses wearing trash bags would crystallize into a chilling realization: the United States was no longer capable of making the basic, everyday items its citizens needed to survive, whether those were phones, computer chips that powered cars, or medical supplies.

The pandemic had exposed that the habits and priorities of American companies, consumers, and politicians were no longer viable. The mood in the country had changed. "What a small, shameful way for a strong nation to falter," wrote New York Times columnist Farhad Manjoo (the same guy who had written the Slate article about American Giant's hoodie all those years ago). "For want of a seventy-five-cent face mask, the kingdom was lost." As it turned out, the electrocharged melt-blown fabric that attracted and filtered microparticles in N95 masks had been developed in the 1990s in a laboratory at the University of Tennessee, Knoxville, by a scientist named Peter Tsai. America couldn't even make a product it had invented. In a widely circulated essay, Marc Andreessen, the billionaire cofounder of the Silicon Valley venture capital firm Andreessen Horowitz, said that the country had foolishly abandoned its role as a builder nation. "We know—and we're experiencing right now!—the strategic problem of relying on offshore manufacturing of key goods," wrote Andreessen on his firm's website, titling his message "It's Time to Build."

In Washington, the laissez-faire attitude toward globalism and deindustrialization that had characterized government policy at the highest levels for decades was getting a rethink, too. The outgoing Trump administration had lobbied to bring back blue-collar factory jobs and slapped tariffs on China. The newly elected Biden administration was handing out tax breaks and incentives to companies to build chip and battery plants in the U.S. "New factories are rising in urban cores and rural fields, desert flats and surf towns," *The Wall Street Journal* reported. As part of a trillion-dollar infrastructure bill in 2021, Congress voted into law the Make PPE in America Act. It was a Berry Amendment for PPE: going forward, the Departments of Homeland Security, Health and Human Services, and Veterans Affairs would be required to buy from domestic manufacturers.

The apparel industry, however, relied almost exclusively on overseas manufacturing and global shipping routes. And when the pandemic hit, the complex supply chains pioneered by Martin Trust and Les Wexner and refined by fast-fashion brands like H&M, which produced its clothing in forty countries around the world, fractured immediately. Early on, the problem for retailers was excess inventory. Soon, the issue would be getting any product at all. With its lower wages relative to China and more conscionable human-rights practices, Vietnam had become the latest destination in the long flight of the needle. A breakout of COVID cases there in the summer of 2021 caused widespread lockdowns. Nike manufactured more than half of its footwear in Vietnam; a third of Gap and Lululemon products were made there. Nike and several other retailers wrote a letter pleading with the White House to fast-track donations of the U.S.-developed COVID-19 vaccine to Southeast Asia so that they could get up and running again. "The health of our industry is directly dependent on the health of Vietnam's industry," the companies wrote in a stunning admission. Many Vietnamese factories remained closed through the fall, and by November, Nike was telling shoppers it didn't have enough sneakers for Christmas.

That same fall, more than sixty container ships idled off the Ports of Long Beach and Los Angeles, the two major U.S. entry points for goods produced in Asia; the boats were unable to unload their cargo. Months earlier, following its strict "zero COVID" policy, the Chinese government had shut down an entire terminal at the Ningbo-Zhoushan Port, among the busiest in the world by measure of cargo tonnage, after a single worker there tested positive for the virus. It caused a chain reaction of shipping buildups and bottlenecks that were worsened by a shortage in the U.S. of workers and truck trailers. The time it took to send Asian-made sneakers or jeans to North America had doubled, from around forty days to eighty. "Supply-chain issues" became the common excuse from out-of-stock retailers (so much so that Jack White even borrowed the phrase for his concert tour), while the flotilla of drifting ships became an enduring image of the pandemic—an absurdist metaphor for globalism's breakdown.

Watching the cargo ships drift in circles and following the happenings in Washington, I wondered if apparel brands that produced overseas would rethink their business model. Would American retailers bring production back home? Could the 2 percent grow to 4 percent or 8 percent or more?

●　●●●●　●

For a while, tracking the industry news, it felt like the American apparel industry was only shrinking. I had been particularly dismayed by the demise of my beloved Woolrich and the closing of its woolen mill, which had happened just as Bayard Winthrop and James McKinnon were reviving flannel.

In September 2018, I read that the company had been sold to a private-equity firm from abroad, L-GAM Advisers. The article said only that the deal signaled a "further step in the globalization process" of the Woolrich brand. The sale, after nearly two centuries of local ownership, came as a shock to me. I wondered how a brand could be "global" when the fabric was milled just twenty miles from where I grew up.

The mill itself told the story.

In the mid-1990s, the mill had still operated two shifts, busily turning out fabric for the spring and fall men's and women's collections, a blanket line, and a "city" line for private-label customers. There was so much work to be done that fabric designer Rob Stuart, who came to Woolrich in 1997, barely slept. Stuart had grown up in Scotland and worked at mills in Europe and the United States. As an outsider, he was struck by the insularity of the place and by the skill of the millworkers. "Some of the guys never left the valley," he said. "They had spent their entire working lives at the mill."

For Woolrich and its customers like me, the mill was both working factory and symbol, featuring prominently in the company's advertising. But inside, it was a different story. The mill had been expanded at various points over the decades, resulting in a mazelike complex with low ceilings and dark corridors. Efficient workflow was impossible, Stuart said, not only because of the lack of logic to the mill's layout but also because of the ancient equipment. The tenter, a machine onto which lengths of washed fabric are hung so they can be heated and set (the origin of the idiom "on tenterhooks"), dated from the 1940s. The millworkers were constantly beset by little technical problems with the machines. When a part broke, a new one had to be specially fabricated for it—the machine makers were long out of business, too.

To modernize the mill would have cost millions, and under the leadership of president and CEO Roz Brayton, the company had decided not to pursue it. The mill's obsolete machinery and expensive workforce meant it could no longer compete with foreign mills. In 2003, Stuart was sent to Shanghai to hand over his designs to a mill there. From that point on, though customers were largely unaware of the change, woolen fabric for Woolrich garments was woven in China.

The mill in Woolrich was left to hobble along with limited-run special projects, like weaving fabric for blankets, making wool for Stetson hats, or doing military contracts under the Berry Amendment. But the Rich family couldn't bring themselves to close the mill. Keeping it going preserved Woolrich's status as a storied American manufacturer.

"Woolrich always wanted to try to make its products in the United States," Brayton's son Nick, a seventh-generation descendant and former president of Woolrich, told me. "We never took the initiative to build a plant in China, for instance. We used third parties. But it impacted margins. It impacted lead times. It definitely hindered our ability to compete with other companies."

Roz would be the last family head of the company who had grown up in the village of Woolrich. He died suddenly of a heart attack in 2007—he was found by his employees in the company fitness room—and after a few interim presidents, the tradition that Woolrich be run by a male Rich descendant resulted in Nick being appointed president in 2012, at the age of thirty-three, and with just a handful of years at the company. It fell to him and an even younger cousin, now serving as vice president, to manage what had become a complicated legacy: a forty-thousand-square-foot mill that had been losing money for years, plus four thousand acres of land surrounding the village and even a hunting lodge. They were also responsible to a hundred or so living descendants of John Rich, spread all over the country, each of whom collected a dividend check. (The days when the family "turned into the business all the earnings of the concern, declaring no dividends," were long past.)

Even with the boost in popularity and sales from the heritage movement, by 2012 Woolrich was in trouble. The company had gone offshore too late to keep up with competitors like Columbia and L. L. Bean, who could outspend Woolrich on marketing and undercut it on price. (In 1998, Columbia went public; by 2005, the stock price had risen 287 percent, and annual sales topped $1 billion.) Under Nick, Woolrich froze its pension plan, ended the dividends, and stopped bidding on unprofitable government contracts to make military uniforms at the mill. There were major layoffs; employees with twenty and thirty years of service were let go. The sewing plant in the nearby town of Jersey Shore, closed during the 2008 downturn, was the last off-site location to go. The mill persevered.

In 2014, amid all the cost cutting, Woolrich opened its first U.S. flagship store, in Manhattan's SoHo neighborhood. The boutique was a short subway ride from my apartment, but I never shopped there. The store sold the European line aimed at the luxury market: cashmere sweaters, work shirts made of recycled melton wool, $1,200 puffer coats. I waited for the clothes to show up at the outlet in Woolrich. Even deeply discounted, they lingered on the racks, too expensive and fashion-forward for the blue-collar workers and hunters from the community. Woolrich seemed caught between its rural Pennsylvania heritage and its more global present and future.

In 2016, Nick Brayton, the Woolrich board, and the living Rich descendants voted to merge Woolrich's U.S. operations with W. P. Lavori, the Italian company that held the license in Europe, and form a new company, Woolrich International. Nick hoped that Lavori would inject cash into the struggling U.S. operation and help build out the brick-and-mortar retail that he believed was necessary for the brand's future.

Around this time, James Welstead, a veteran textile designer and former millowner from Scotland—he and Rob Stuart attended textile college together—was brought over to Woolrich by Lavori as a consultant to assess the factory. When I asked about his first impression of the place, Welstead laughed and quoted the English poet William Blake, calling it "a dark, satanic mill."

Still, Welstead believed the mill was a priceless asset. He thought Woolrich would be making a strategic error by closing it, a point he said he argued to Lavori executives. "If you go into any store of Woolrich, whether it's Tokyo, Milan, Paris, New York, they've got it written up on the wall: 'We proudly cherish our American craft textile heritage.' Nowadays, people want transparency in the supply chain. They want actual, *real* authenticity, not bullshit authenticity. And you're going to close the mill?"

Welstead proposed a $6 million plan to save the mill. He envisioned turning part of it into a museum and then creating a new minimill on-site, with modern looms and an energetic young workforce. But after the merger, production slowed further, and Welstead saw the writing on the wall. "Fashion companies like W. P. Lavori don't produce. They don't like making things," he said. "They especially don't like old mills that soak up money."

Just ten months after the merger, Cristina Calori, Lavori's president and now the majority shareholder of Woolrich, changed course and sold all her shares to L-GAM, the private-equity firm. L-GAM worked in partnership with the Princely Family of Liechtenstein, the tiny European monarchy bordering Switzerland whose per-capita GDP ranked second in the world. The family was surprised, but it accepted the price L-GAM offered for the outstanding stock—more than $200 a share. For 188 years, Woolrich had been headquartered in north-central Pennsylvania and run by a Rich. Going forward, the Europeans would be in charge, and the family would exit the company altogether.

Three months after L-GAM took control, in December 2018, the oldest running U.S. woolen mill, the original temple of American flannel, was closed permanently.

The summer of 2020 brought the end of another historic American clothing manufacturer.

Brooks Brothers had been one of the companies that pitched in to make PPE at the beginning of the pandemic, though not as a member of Parkdale's coalition. At its three factories, America's oldest clothing company, two centuries in business, made medical gowns and surgical masks with a union workforce. But just a few months later, Brooks Brothers filed for bankruptcy protection. The company announced that it would close one-fifth of its retail stores in North America and all three U.S. factories.

Both Abraham Lincoln and Barack Obama had worn Brooks Brothers overcoats on their inauguration days, and the label's preppy clothes "personified East Coast success in the Kennedy vein," as two *New York Times* reporters wrote. Perhaps because of that long history, or maybe because of the widespread aura of grief and mourning in the country during that plague year, Brooks Brothers received an outpouring of tributes and farewells in the media. The journalist Matthew Walther, writing for *The Week*, saw in the bankruptcy a greater story of loss. "The lamentable decline of American textile manufacturing has followed the same pattern as the collapse of so many industries," he wrote. "We now live in a world in which nearly everything is either a piece of junk made by wage slaves in China or Southeast Asia or a luxury good. Until recently, Brooks Brothers was a rare example of something that stood in between."

It appeared that Brooks Brothers had been done in by the very same cultural trends boosting American Giant. It sold suits, ties, and dress shoes at a time when men wore hoodies and Nike Air Force 1s. But to close followers like Derek Guy, who writes the menswear blog *Die, Workwear!*, the bankruptcy was the inevitable result of a brand that had lost its way. Brooks Brothers had "abandoned its American roots," Guy wrote, chasing trends like stretch denim and outsourcing a lot of its production to overseas factories. Under the ownership of Claudio Del Vecchio, a billionaire Italian industrialist who bought the company in 2001, the label had gone from fewer than a dozen stores in U.S. cities to more than five hundred globally, and to sustain that growth, it ran constant sales and sold poorer-quality shirts in three-packs, which ultimately tarnished Brooks Brothers' legacy of quality.

To Michael Williams, the founder of the men's style site A Continuous Lean, the company had committed the cardinal sin— choosing the mass market over having great products and a few great stores. "Maybe no one stopped to think about the fact that Brooks Brothers wasn't meant to be a two-billion-dollar brand," Williams wrote on his blog in a post that asked, "What is the measure of a good company?" "J. Crew and Gap do that kind of volume—why would anyone want to end up like that?" Brooks Brothers was soon bought out of bankruptcy for $325 million by the mall developer Simon Property Group and the brand management company Authentic Brands, owner of such mass retailers as Nine West and Forever 21. Authentic Brands also owned the image rights of Elvis Presley and Marilyn Monroe. Like them, Brooks Brothers was a world-famous name, ripe to be licensed and merchandised.

Brooks Brothers' Garland shirt factory was renowned for its quality, but there was little chance it would be bought and reopened by another brand. The only thing harder than owning an apparel factory was owning a union-run factory; not even Bayard was willing to take that on. And while Brooks was not likely to ever manufacture in America again, there was scant evidence that big, successful apparel brands like Nike, Levi's, and Ralph Lauren were now more willing to, either. The exception was New Balance, the only major American footwear brand that produced most of its shoes domestically. New Balance opened a fifth U.S. factory in Massachusetts in 2022 and announced a $65 million expansion of its existing Skowhegan, Maine, plant that would increase production to more than a million shoes per year and create two hundred jobs. Otherwise, Big Apparel seemed absent from the national conversation around reshoring.

I thought of something that I'd heard over and over from people I'd spoken to about American-made clothing—"It's never coming back"—and had to wonder if they were right.

It was when I was most in doubt that I received an email from Amy Williams, the CEO of Citizens of Humanity, the L.A.-based premium-denim label. She had heard about my interest in domestically made clothing and wanted to tell me about a project the brand was working on. We met at a Manhattan café a few months later, when she was in the city for New York Fashion Week and running all over town to appointments.

Amy Williams was in her fifties, with a cool California demeanor despite the stresses of being a fashion CEO. An industry veteran, she had lived through the same profound changes that manufacturers had experienced, but from the retail side. Having gone to work for the Gap in 1989, she could remember when the label still produced a lot of its clothes stateside. As the head of product development and design for women's denim at that time, she worked with small-town factory owners. "I was going to the mills, choosing the fabric, doing wash development," said Amy. "I'd go to Mississippi, Kentucky, and Tennessee to work with our sewing factories. Kentucky Apparel— we were doing at least one hundred thousand units a week there. That was just the women's division." But by the time she left the Gap, in 2003, the retailer was sourcing its clothes from more than a thousand factories in forty-two countries.

Citizens of Humanity was a very different business. Founded in 2003 by Jerome Dahan, a French denim connoisseur, and Michael Glasser, a designer, the label grew out of the "premium" jeans trend of the era, when labels like 7 For All Mankind (where Dahan was also the creative partner), Diesel, Rogan, and G-Star added studs, grommets, pocket details, and elaborate washes and treatments to denim and sold jeans for $200 and up. At Citizens of Humanity, the emphasis on design and quality meant that the label operated a lot like a European luxury brand, keeping tight control of its manufacturing and supply chain.

In 2011, a year after Amy joined the label, Citizens built a vertical production factory in downtown L.A., where the cutting and sewing of garments could be done. This added to its industrial laundry nearby. The designers worked closely with the seamstresses and patternmakers on a first-name basis. If, say, they had an idea for a pocket shape, they could sit next to the sewer and explain how they'd like that pocket to look. They could visit the laundry and see how the first samples of a new wash came out. It made for a collaborative process that reduced waste. They didn't have to work a year out, as was the norm for offshore manufacture. "We can produce clothes in L.A. in eight to ten weeks and ship them out," Amy said. "We save carbon emissions by manufacturing here. We do much of our prototyping in Los Angeles. We sample less than any place I've ever been."

The project that she wanted to tell me about involved regenerative agriculture—a sustainable farming practice that involves mulching the soil instead of tilling it and planting cover crops in the offseason. These practices, among others, restore soil health, secure carbon in the ground, and save groundwater. In a way, regenerative farming is a step beyond organic.

Citizens of Humanity had put together a group of six farmers across the U.S., from California to Louisiana, to grow the cotton for its jeans in this regenerative way. The cotton crop for that year was already planted, Amy said, and the farmers were on track to produce a million pounds—enough cotton to make about five hundred thousand pairs of jeans. That amounted to 25 percent of the company's total production of garments for the coming year. Ultimately, the label wanted to make all its clothes using regeneratively grown cotton.

At present, Amy added, Citizens of Humanity was also testing whether regenerative cotton, which has a different texture and character than cotton grown traditionally, could be woven into jean pocketing. Her partner in the project was a familiar name: James McKinnon of Cotswold.

It had been a while since I was last in touch with James, but he was still hustling and making it rain. In March 2020, within days of the first COVID deaths and the lockdowns, he had created a whole new division of Cotswold—Saxon Shield, a medical brand that made PPE for FEMA and other government agencies. Cotswold was well-positioned to supply the new market: it already made nonwovens used in medical applications like blood-pressure cuffs. It also had a government-procurement division that bid on federal contracts, and, thanks to an earlier acquisition by James, the company owned TexTest Laboratories, a government-certified materials testing lab in Georgia. "At Cotswold, we're textile engineers. That's what we are," James said when I called him. "From fiber to chemistry to constructions to end-use scenarios and supply chains—we figure it out."

Amy knew James through mutual industry connections and had

heard about his role in making American Giant's flannel shirt. She admired his gumption. "He wants to do things that no one else can do," she said. "He told us, 'I love a challenge.'" James introduced Amy to a contact at Parkdale Mills, and Parkdale agreed to spin the regenerative cotton for Citizens of Humanity. Now, their knits could be fully manufactured in the United States, from U.S.-grown cotton to spinning at Parkdale, knitting in L.A., and cutting, washing, and dyeing in California as well. The label's denim would use this U.S.-grown regenerative cotton, too, but for now it would have to be sent to Turkey and Italy to be woven, as no U.S. mill had the ability to weave and dye the stretch denim Citizens used.

In 2017, Gary Freedman, the label's chief operating officer, Amy, and some other executives had bought Citizens of Humanity from cofounder Jerome Dahan and the private-equity firm that had purchased a stake in the company. In effect, Amy was betting her financial future on American manufacturing and sustainable practices like regenerative farming. I asked her why, and she mentioned her twin daughters, now thirteen. "They still care about how the clothes make them look and feel, but there's a new level of scrutiny," she said. "They're so much more inquisitive about 'Where does this come from?' The post-COVID era and this question of where products are from is challenging us to go deeper."

She also spoke of the sadness she felt at watching companies like Graniteville, Burlington, and Cone go offshore or out of business as apparel retailers moved to outsourcing during the 1990s. "I'd travel to these places, and the garment factory was the only place to work in town," Amy said. "We feel a responsibility to keep jobs in the United States. Growing cotton, weaving cotton, and sewing and laundering denim here. Jobs, quality, sustainability in terms of the American economy. And personal pride. You feel good about the choices that you're making every day as a businessperson when you get to do things that hold all of those values in place."

Amy spoke about the apparel business with such clarity and common sense that I had to remind myself that what she was saying was not accepted practice but, in the broader industry, still heresy.

The energy around American-made apparel, the innovation from new and growing factories, I now saw, would not come from the big brands, which were far too reliant on cheap foreign labor and beholden to quarterly earnings and the imperative to move massive product. The energy and innovation would come from the people who'd kept U.S. apparel manufacturing going all these years— mavericks who did it for reasons of family and community, for the satisfaction and pride of making things, out of a set of personal values or from sheer stubbornness. There seemed to be a constantly replenishing supply of such people willing to give it a go.

Sasha Koehn and Erik Allen Ford, the founders of Buck Mason, started out of a garage space in Venice, California, in 2013. They received their education in the apparel business by knocking on factory doors in downtown Los Angeles, soaking up knowledge that people still working in the clothing game were happy to share. They sold $30 premium T-shirts made of slub cotton and $140 canvas work pants, gaining a loyal following among conscientious, thoughtful consumers who had grown up on the internet reading blogs like *ACL*. After hiring factories onshore and abroad, they began dreaming of building their own. They longed to be able to own and refine every step of the process.

In 2022, they heard about a recently closed apparel factory that was for sale in Mohnton, Pennsylvania, near Reading, an area with a history of garment production and a sense of pride and dignity in the craft. The factory had been producing knitwear since the 1950s. The sewers working there had something like eighteen years of experience, on average. The business also came with a fabric mill in a separate building—another dream.

It was a fully functional version of what Sasha and Erik had aspired to build one day, and in short order they bought the factory and rehired half of its laid-off employees. They liked their chances as an American manufacturer competing in the global market.

"You've got some of the best long-staple cotton in the world grown in the U.S.," Erik said. "You've got great spinners where you can spin that cotton. We can now knit that product—we have the expertise. We can cut, sew, dye that product. You never have to pay an import tax or global travel. We can rival China, Vietnam, Peru. We can rival all the competing countries."

Up in Connecticut, meanwhile, a new product was coming off the looms at a woolen mill dating from the 1850s. Or, rather, an old product—a wool and mohair "Chatham" blanket. It was the brainchild of an industrial designer named Alex Chatham, whose great-great-grandfather, Alexander Chatham, a gristmill worker in North

Carolina, had founded a company called Chatham Manufacturing after the Civil War. Chatham Manufacturing grew to become one of the largest wool blanket manufacturers in the world during the years preceding and following World War II. Alex had grown up in lower Manhattan hearing about the business, which had passed out of family ownership in the 1980s and then closed. In 2017, when he was in his midthirties and living in Brooklyn, and inspired in large part by the heritage movement, he decided to revive the label.

At the time, there were perhaps three places left in the country that could weave a traditional wool blanket with the napped finish that Alex wanted. Woolrich was out—they closed their mill soon after he contacted the company. Minnesota's Faribault Woolen Mill declined to do private-label. Pendleton, the last option, had high factory minimums that were prohibitive for a fledgling business.

Years passed. Alex kept pursuing his idea. He hired a Chinese mill to make a few blankets as samples. The Chinese mill had low minimums and a quick turnaround, but the quality wasn't that great, and anyway, it didn't feel right. "To rebuild the brand the way that I wanted to do it, it had to be made in America," Alex said. "It had to be this irrational way. There was never a moment that I thought I would make them outside the U.S."

All the obstacles only spurred Alex on. Finally, he heard about a mill in Connecticut, American Woolen, that for many years had been owned by the Italian luxury goods company Loro Piana. It was now under new ownership, roaring back to life weaving rugged woolens and fine worsteds. Alex hired American Woolen to produce his singular product, which he began selling through his website and in partnership with Martha Stewart's American Made e-commerce site. He designed a second blanket, and a third, and a fourth. Alex admired the ethos of the heritage movement—to make a timeless, durable product. "It was kind of in opposition to my day job," creating new products, he said. "There are products that are eternal. They don't need to be revolutionary. They just need to be excellent."

＊ ＊＊＊ ＊

It was the sort of sentiment that Michael Williams would have expressed on his blog. But after 2015, Williams had pulled back from posting regularly. He felt that the whole heritage thing had been reduced to a trendy look, stripped of its deeper meaning. He'd be out somewhere and see someone and instantly peg them for an *ACL* reader. "They're wearing a buffalo-plaid shirt and wax canvas jacket and rugged boots and, like, a Stetson hat, with a crazy beard," he said, exasperated. "I would be, like, 'Don't talk to me. I can't handle this.'"

He had also been put off by the takeover of "made in America" by political extremists. Like many Americans, Williams believed that outsourcing had destroyed whole regions and communities, but Trump with his trade wars, untruthfulness, and chaotic governing was like having the worst possible spokesperson for the movement. Up until then, Williams always thought the American-made movement would continue to trend upward as more people became wise to the value and logic behind it. "But when Trump got elected, it got co-opted by this far-right group," he said. "It got tainted. I thought 'made in the U.S.A.' was probably dead at that point. I never thought it would recover."

The pandemic changed that, and it changed Williams, too. He reengaged with his blog in spring 2020, writing a series of posts that, like Marc Andreessen's "It's Time to Build" essay, took the country to task for turning away from manufacturing and building. "I was infuriated by the fact that we can't make N95 masks," Williams said. "It goes to show we're just inept. We're this limp shell of a country. We don't have the machines. Everything is so dependent on other countries."

From his home in Los Angeles, Williams watched like everyone else as most of the economy ground to a halt during the pandemic. Dire as things were, however, he figured that the businesses he'd written about and championed for so long would be okay financially. Small American brands like Alden and Rancourt were used to being on the defensive, and they were run conservatively. Williams regarded them a bit like exotic plants growing in the desert—they had adapted to life with very little water.

But in June, he called Kyle Rancourt to catch up and see how the shoe company was faring during the pandemic.

"Dude, what's up with your business?" Williams asked.

"We have no business," Kyle replied. "It's really, really bad."

A bunch of wholesale orders had been canceled or postponed, while customer orders through the Rancourt website had dropped to zero. Now Mike and Kyle were facing the very real possibility of having to lay off their workers.

Williams lent his marketing skills, helping Kyle hatch a plan for a crowdfunded project. Rancourt would offer its retail customers wholesale pricing on some of its bestselling shoes, like the classic ranger moc and the beefroll penny loafer. By meeting minimum order quantities, the factory could use batch production to make the program efficient and profitable. Williams did free PR for Rancourt around the crowdfund, asking friends and fashion influencers to share it, calling in a lot of favors and doing everything he could to get eyeballs on it. He promoted it to his readers on *ACL*, with its mailing list of thirty thousand subscribers.

Essentially, Rancourt was making the same plea for support and call to action that the Crafted with Pride ads had once made. This time, the response from customers was overwhelming. Rancourt's website was flooded with orders. Within days, Mike and Kyle had filled enough orders to keep going deep into 2020, long enough to get the business through the worst of the shutdown. A shoe factory in Maine was at full capacity for months, in the middle of a pandemic.

One of the people who bought Rancourt shoes was Brian Davis, the dealer in vintage menswear. The pair of moccasins he purchased was a rare buy for him during quarantine. It was an investment in quality, and in American workers. "In that factory, I bet you have people who have been doing the same thing every day for decades," Davis said. "You're not telling me that if you moved all that manufacturing offshore, that someone is going to be able to sew as good on their first day as the person doing it for forty years."

When I returned to Lewiston in July 2022, there were significantly more cars in Rancourt's employee parking lot; the company had added a dozen workers in the previous two years. Inside, a group of well-dressed tourists were buying shoes in the factory store off the lobby. The factory itself was hopping. In 2020 and 2021, the company had seen its two best years ever for revenue, Kyle told me. "Our online business is the biggest it's ever been. Then you couple that with the growth of private label—making shoes for other brands." Handsewn shoes were back in style; the winds of fashion had shifted in Rancourt's favor. But that didn't explain it entirely. In the wake of the pandemic, people were more interested in U.S. manufacturing, and apparel labels were responding to it. "You get merchandising and design teams at these big brands wanting to have something in their collection to represent 'made in America,'" Kyle said. "So they're coming to us because there are very few options left to get shoes made here."

Out on the factory floor, in the hand-sewing department, Jeff and Jewel had a new colleague. A middle-aged man from Angola with a shaved head and thick-framed glasses stood at the workbench in front of Jeff's. Joao Kalukembiko had come to the United States in 2016, with his wife and child. In New York City, where he initially lived, a fellow immigrant told Joao about Maine. "You can go there—everything is going to be perfect," the friend told him.

He worked first at a Dunkin' Donuts. Then he heard about Rancourt through Lewiston's African immigrant community. Kyle liked Joao's positive personality and hired him on that basis. He and his dad knew that, these days, they weren't going to find people who knew how to make shoes. Instead, they decided they would train new workers like Joao.

After trying a few different jobs, Joao proved to be good at stitching soles for Rancourt's sneaker line, work that required hand-eye coordination and close attention to detail. One day, Joao mentioned to Mike that he wanted to try hand sewing. Mike got him training with the veterans, and unlike everyone else who had tried it, he did well and stuck with it.

By the time I arrived, Joao had been doing the job for more than a year—long enough, by local tradition, to call himself a hand sewer.

For Michael Williams, helping Rancourt through a make-or-break moment had been one of the most satisfying moments of his career. "A lot of times, I think I'm just this marketing guy. I just make people buy more shit. It's hard to reconcile that sometimes," he said. "But then you get to do something like that, and this factory is at full capacity. That's beautiful."

● ●━● ◑

Here were smaller, independent brands innovating and investing in domestic manufacturing at a time of great uncertainty, while their mass-market competitors were willing to tolerate any number of logistical problems and customer complaints to keep outsourcing. Owning a factory and making great products at home, it struck me, was not a decision that a company or its leaders made because of a pandemic or changing political winds or other external events. It was a way of thinking about the world, an inner disposition.

If there was anyone who exemplified that inner disposition, it was Gina Locklear. Not that it made for easy decisions. After the stress and worry she'd faced with Vance's semiretirement, Gina had considered a radical new plan. She would open an office in Birmingham and move her business there. She would quit manufacturing at her family's mill and instead hire one of the remaining mills in Fort Payne to make her socks. She would ditch the long commute and be free of the constant headaches and worries of running a factory.

The plan came with trade-offs. That camellia flower sock, the one she'd sampled over and over until she'd fine-tuned the few stitched lines and arrived at the perfect color combination—you couldn't do that if you contracted with a private-label manufacturer. To get the best quality, you had to be *right there* on the factory floor, every day, overseeing production.

Gina thought long and hard about giving up the mill. In the end, she couldn't do it. She decided she had to find a way to keep her operation going.

The trials of the past year—and the eleven before that—had not broken her. Quite the opposite. "I'm never going to give up on the sock business. No matter what. I've spent too much of my life trying to grow this," Gina told me.

In her search for a way forward, Gina had come to understand something about herself. "I'm not a sock seller," she said with resolve. "I'm a *maker*. It's hard every day. But I still love it. It's what I want to do forever."

Acknowledgments

This book grew from a series of stories about clothing manufacturing that I wrote for *The New York Times*. I'm grateful to the editors who greenlit those articles and shepherded them into print—namely, Alexandra Jacobs, Jim Windolf, and Stuart Emmrich—and additionally grateful to the *Times* for being a world-class institution for a feature reporter to practice the craft. Thanks also to Stella Bugbee for supporting my book leave.

Jim Windolf, Brian Raftery, Karen Gordon, and Emily Nemens generously read early versions of this book and offered insightful improvements. In Emily's case, she rolled up her sleeves and helped me wrestle a difficult first draft into submission.

Lauren Dorr lent her experience as a fashion designer to proofread the technical language. My family gave me the time to write and emotional support—and in the case of my parents, good company on shopping trips to Woolrich. Thanks to PJ Mark at Janklow & Nesbit for his wise counsel including the suggestion for this book's title. I appreciate the work of Shailyn Tavella, Catalina Trigo, and the whole Riverhead team.

ACKNOWLEDGMENTS

Finally, and above all, a big heartfelt thanks to Rebecca Saletan, who believed in the idea for this book and agreed to publish it. Throughout the writing and editing process, Becky was always encouraging, enthusiastic, undaunted, and brilliant on the page. In other words, a dream editor.